T0277994

# Europe and the End of Medieval Japan

# PAST IMPERFECT

**See further**
www.arc-humanities.org/our-series/pi

# Europe and the End of Medieval Japan

**Mark Hudson**

**British Library Cataloguing in Publication Data**
A catalogue record for this book is available from the British Library

ISBN (PB): 9781802701838
e-ISBN (PDF): 9781802702972
e-ISBN (EPUB): 9781802702989


**www.arc-humanities.org**
Printed and bound in the UK (by CPI Group [UK] Ltd), USA (by Bookmasters), and elsewhere using print-on-demand technology.

# Contents

# List of Illustrations

*For Danièle*

# Preface

Readers familiar with my earlier writings may initially be surprised at the subject of this book. My previous research has focused mainly on Neolithic and Bronze Age Japan, with some excursions into the medieval Ryukyus and Hokkaido, the islands at the south and north of the Japanese archipelago. That work has attempted to provide a more global approach to Japanese history, writing against the grain of the isolationist views so common in the literature. The concept of premodern globalization has seemed to me to be a useful perspective in this endeavour. There were three phases when Japan was particularly influenced by global forces: the Bronze Age, the so-called "Christian Century" of the late sixteenth to early seventeenth centuries, and the Meiji to Showa eras (1868–1989). While several of my recent publications have focused on the first of these phases, the present volume considers the second as the time when Europe first came into direct conversation with Japan.

This book was made possible in the first instance by the undergraduate education in Asian history I received at the School of Oriental and African Studies. My teachers—William Atwell, Helen Ballhatchet, William Beasley, K. N. Chaudhuri, Michael Cook, and David Morgan among others—provided an exciting yet durable "big picture" framework. In Japan, Michael Cooper helped me publish my first academic article and stimulated my interest in the issues considered here. More recently, I thank Katarina Šukelj for discussions on Japanese nationalism and historiography. Rafael Abad de los Santos Danièle Martin, Keiko Matsumoto, Peter Matthews, Irene Muñoz Fernández, Martine Robbeets, Tim Screech, Travis Seifman, Hiroto Takamiya, and Royall Tyler graciously replied to questions on aspects of the text. I am also grateful to Brigitte Hofmann and Kristin Starkloff, dedicated librarians of the Max Planck Institute of Geoanthropology. Last but not least, I express my thanks to the anonymous reviewer and to Anna Henderson, Tania Colwell, Laura Macy, and the rest of the Arc Humanities team.

Following the *Past Imperfect* style, footnotes are kept to a minimum, but included for archaeological and scientific studies. Works listed in Further Reading are cited in short form in footnotes. Japanese names are rendered with family name first prior to 1868, but in the European style thereafter.

Chapter I

# Positioning Late Medieval Japan: An Introduction

This book looks at the century of dynamic change between the end of the Middle Ages and the onset of the early modern era in the Japanese Islands. This period of transition from the late sixteenth to the early seventeenth centuries has some-times been labelled the "Christian Century" because it also saw the arrival of European missionaries and merchants in Japan. Although this label is often criticized for its perceived Eurocentric bias, the present volume uses recent writings on premodern globalizations to attempt a re-evaluation of the role played by Europe at the time. The book re-thinks the Christian Century from three perspectives: religion, violence, and cultural exchange.

In order to understand the controversies surrounding the Christian Century concept, it is useful to start with some historiography. If national identity is often refracted through particular historical events or processes, one such lens in Japan has been the nation's relationship with the West and modernity, a connection contrasted to earlier links with the Sinocentric East Asian world. Tension between "West" and "East" remains a recurring feature in Japanese letters. A nativist view of Japanese uniqueness was expounded during the early modern Tokugawa period (1603-1868). The growth of Japan's overseas empire from the late nineteenth century was, by contrast, supported by ideas that linked the roots of the nation with its Asian neighbours—while still insisting on the superiority of the Japanese race. Defeat in 1945 opened the field to a plethora of inventive theories on Japanese origins and history. Despite the diversity of ideas now on offer, however, there was one thing almost all authors agreed on: that the essential nature of Japan was to be found in features in opposition to wartime agendas—peace, social harmony, open capitalism, and democracy. These features, it was suggested, derived from Japan's native endowments rather than from contact with the outside.

Post-war re-evaluation of Japan's past aligned closely with the values ostensibly espoused by the United States of America, which led the Allied Occupation of Japan until 1952 (or 1972 in the Ryukyu Islands). Japan's remarkable economic success after 1945 offered a pathway that was not Western or Communist but a third way for non-aligned countries. America looked to Japan as a Cold War ally just as Japan demonstrated American ability to rebuild a nation in its own image. As a result, academic research on Japan in North America became focused on modernization, which the United States considered itself as the paragon. "Old Japan" was of interest primarily as a baseline of traditional life, initially traced back only a few centuries to the Tokugawa. If historical evaluation of premodern Japan was over-determined by modernity, the initial reaction was entirely negative, viewing Tokugawa as a backward, feudal burden impeding progress. The narrative of America's fraternal "opening" of Japan in the nineteenth century required previous closure. Yet Japan's very success in modernization led to the invocation of Tokugawa as a traditional but nevertheless advanced civilization that had developed in splendid isolation from the West. Dismayed by the ostentatious crassness of modernity, especially in its vulgar American manifestations, many Japanese intellectuals came to regard Tokugawa as the home of an authentic, because *pre*-Western Japanese identity.

The post-war focus on Japan's internal evolution was consistent with Marxism as well as modernization theory: both emphasized historical progress generated *within* Japanese society. While Marxism was the dominant frame of reference for Japanese scholars in the early post-war decades, by the

1980s Japan's growing economic power and the end of the Cold War were associated with the revival of more nationalistic interpretations. While down-playing outside influences on Japan's past remained a standard incantation, some writers began to re-cycle wartime Pan-Asianist ideas. Yoshinori Yasuda brought a new twist to the North–South dualism originally developed by Kurakichi Shiratori (1865–1942) as an antidote to the East–West division he thought denigrated Japan. Japan's true culture, argued Yasuda, originated in the peaceful rice farming and fishing cultures of southern China and Southeast Asia. Yasuda also returned to the anti-Christian polemics that had accompanied state-building in late nineteenth and early twentieth-century Japan.[1]

Emphasis on the internal evolution of Japan, be it through Marxism or modernization theory, could not deny *all* external impacts. As a result, the history of the archipelago is typically portrayed through fundamental isolation punctuated by a few phases of intense contact with the outside. While the most authentic features of Japanese culture developed during isolation, measured exposure to the outside was necessary for Japan to "catch up" with certain social and technological changes. The arrival of agriculture and metal-working in the Bronze Age Yayoi period (ca. 1000 BC–AD 250) was one such punctuation, as was the spread of Buddhism and T'ang court culture in the eighth century. Numerous historians and archaeologists have nevertheless argued that even these punctuations reflect the unusual ability of the Japanese themselves to adopt outside customs.

The idea of punctuations has been applied to Japan's so-called "opening" to the West. The first stage saw contacts with western Europe, above all Iberia, during the "Christian Century" of the late sixteenth to early seventeenth centuries. The second stage in the mid-nineteenth century was led ini-

---

I For a critical discussion of Yasuda's work, which includes several anti-Christian polemics, see my *Conjuring Up Prehistory: Landscape and the Archaic in Japanese Nationalism* (Oxford: Archaeopress, 2021).

tially by American naval squadrons. Following Ronald Toby's description of the first stage as the "Iberian irruption," we might term the second the American or "Yankee irruption."[2] These two irruptions have been approached in very different ways. The first is widely dismissed with respect to its long-term impacts; marked as Catholic and therefore anti-modern, it represented a false start. Contact with Europe might even be considered to have resulted in a reactionary re-feudalization rather than growth towards modernization. If modernization was the endpoint of a series of progressive historical stages, the Christian Century held an ambivalent position in such imaginings, apparently confirming the significance of the authentic opening of Japan by a modern (and Protestant) America.

The term "Christian Century" was introduced in C. R. Boxer's 1951 book *The Christian Century in Japan, 1549–1650*. Murdoch and Yamagata's 1903 *A History of Japan during the Century of Early Foreign Intercourse, 1542–1651* had set the scene for the periodization. Boxer's chronology began when Basque Jesuit Francis Xavier (1506–1552) reached the port of Kagoshima in southern Kyushu (Map 1.1). An alternative date would be the arrival of a group of Portuguese sailors at Tanegashima Island in 1543. The first edict aimed at expelling Iberian missionaries from Japan was issued as early as 1587, but it was not until the 1640s, after a series of brutal persecutions, that all practising Christians were banned from the country or forced underground. While the Christian Century has primarily been approached as a Catholic phenomenon, the Dutch and English also established a presence in Japan. Englishman William Adams (1564–1620) reached Kyushu in 1600 as pilot of a Dutch ship. A Dutch trading post was established at Hirado in 1609, followed closely by the English in

---

**2** Ronald Toby, *Engaging the Other: "Japan" and its Alter Egos, 1550–1850* (Leiden: Brill, 2019). New Englanders, notably Matthew Perry, Ernest Fenollosa, Edward Morse, Horace Capron, and William Clark, played an inordinate role in early Meiji. Predictably, Americans were soon calling the Japanese the "Yankees of Asia."

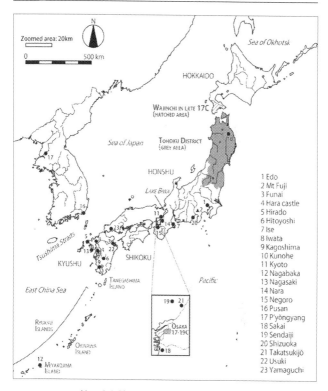

Map 1.1 Places mentioned in the text.
Map by Junzō Uchiyama. Used by permission.

1613. The English abandoned Hirado in 1623 and the Dutch were forced to move to Dejima, an artificial island in Nagasaki Bay, in 1641. Although the Dutch continued to trade from Nagasaki throughout the Tokugawa period, the practice of Christianity was prohibited in Japan until 1873.

The 1543 arrival of Portuguese sailors at Tanegashima is usually described as the first visit by Europeans to Japanese waters. However, various inconsistencies in the sources suggest a context of earlier exploration, something that would

not be unexpected since Europeans had long wanted to dis-
cover Marco Polo's famed "Zipangu."[3] In the Archive of the
Indies in Seville there is a Spanish document titled "Brief
Description of Japan," which describes the land and customs
of Kyushu. It has been suggested that this text can be linked
with Andrés de Urdaneta (1508–1568), a Basque explorer and
Augustinian friar who took part in the Loaísa expedition to
the Spice Islands (1525–1536). From Ternate, Urdaneta was
sent on various reconnaissance missions, and it has been
proposed that he visited Japan in the early 1530s.[4] Further
research is needed, but this document is more likely a Spanish summary of the well-known 1547 description of Kyushu by
Portuguese sea-captain Jorge Álvares.

Most historians have dismissed the Christian Century as
a short anomaly in the main current of Japan's past. While
conversions were made, it is suggested that the Japanese did
not really understand the foreign religion. George Sansom
speculated that "Perhaps it was because [the] early [Japa-
nese] converts did not fully understand what their creed
entailed that the Jesuits made such rapid progress," though
he acknowledged a few converts being "genuine to the point
of fanaticism." Christianity, for Sansom, could even be seen
as "one of those [foreign] crazes which have often swept
over Japan." Such comments reflect an Orientalist trope used
to explain why modern Japan did not fit the image of the
Unchanging East. According to Sansom, "Nowhere have men
more eagerly, nay recklessly, leaped to welcome new things
and new notions."[5] In other words, Japan was not static but

**3** For a recent analysis of the sources on Tanegashima, see Susan
Tsumura, "'A Ship Arrived from an Unknown Country on a Fire-Bird
Day': Another Look at the *Teppōki*," *Journal of Asian Humanities at
Kyushu University* 9 (2024): 37–50.

**4** José Ramón de Miguel Bosch, "Andrés de Urdaneta y Japón,"
*Revisita Santa Ana* (2007): 28–31, www.andresurdaneta.org
/urdaneta500/de/andres-de-urdaneta-y-japon-2144.
asp?nombre=2144&cod=2144&sesion=1, accessed August 7, 2024.

**5** Mirroring earlier comments by Engelbert Kaempfer (1651–1716),

its change was impulsive. Another common argument is that Japanese élites toyed with Christianity not through any real religious conviction but as a way to access trade and European technology, especially guns.

A conspicuous element of the historiography of the Christian Century is an anti-Catholic tone especially common in earlier English-language writings. American diplomat and historian George Kerr claimed that Tokugawa Ieyasu was "tolerant of the Protestant English and Dutch traders, who were indifferent to religious interests"; by contrast, "Japan's rulers had ample reason to dislike and mistrust the Spanish and Portuguese missionaries, who were trouble-makers." Sansom explained that, "Cruelly intolerant these Jesuits may have been, but they kept a severe rule, they had breeding and learning and a touch of haughtiness—all qualities that were admired in feudal Japan." Protestant writers have played down the impact of the early Catholic missions. In *The Mikado's Empire*, first published in 1876, Pennsylvania educator and Reformed minister William Griffis insisted that "The influence of a century of Papal Christianity in Japan on the national ethics and character was *nil*." Sansom claimed that potatoes and tobacco were better appreciated by the Japanese than Catholic doctrines.[6]

Although there is a growing specialist literature on the Christian Century, the era receives little attention in many English language histories. Richard Mason and John Caiger's *A History of Japan* (1973, revised 1997) insists that "neither Christianity nor foreign trade emerged as central issues of Japanese history in the sixteenth century." Karl Friday's

---

Sansom also proposed that "there is something in the Japanese character which responds to the Latin temperament"; George Sansom, *Japan: A Short Cultural History*, rev. ed. (Rutland: Tuttle, 1973), 435, 417–21.

**6** George H. Kerr, *Okinawa: The History of Island People* (Rutland: Tuttle, 1958), 169, 173; William E. Griffis, *The Mikado's Empire: A History of Japan from the Mythological Age to Meiji Era*, 8th ed. (New York: ICG Muse, 2000 [1895]), 285; Sansom, *Japan: A Short Cultural History*, 417–21.

edited *Japan Emerging: Premodern History to 1850* (2012)—perhaps the best introduction to its subject in recent years—is unusual in including several chapters that discuss the Christian Century, though often in a way that makes it difficult to connect broader trends. Brett Walker devotes a whole chapter to "Japan's encounter with Europe, 1543–1640" in his *Concise History of Japan* (2015). The influence of this encounter on subsequent Tokugawa foreign policy is emphasized, as is the role of technology, including glass lenses in generating new ways of seeing the world. The *Routledge Handbook of Premodern Japanese History* (2017), again edited by Friday, covers events up to 1600 and contains an excellent overview of the role of firearms in late medieval warfare, but only one incidental mention of Christianity.

There are two main reasons why historians have resisted the term "Christian Century." First, it seems to portray Japan's past through a suspiciously European and Christian lens. John Hall began Volume 4 of the *Cambridge History of Japan* by announcing he would avoid the term Christian Century "because of its possible overemphasis on the foreign factor." From the 1970s Japanese historians have de-coupled the sixteenth and seventeenth centuries from "global" trends—understood as meaning a focus on Europe via the trope of the "Age of Discovery." In contrast, new writings placed Japan in its East Asian context. Yasunori Arano approached the Century through the "*wakō* phenomenon," referring to "Japanese" pirate-traders who in fact derived from various regions of East and Southeast Asia. Drawing on the work of Arano, Ronald Toby's influential 1984 book *State and Diplomacy in Early Modern Japan* had the radical subtitle *Asia in the Development of the Tokugawa Bakufu*. Toby attempted to position Japan at the centre of its own world rather than as a periphery of China or Europe. My endeavour here is to strive for a *global*—rather than a Japanocentric or Eurocentric—perspective, while accepting the existence of numerous social, religious and political differences between the actors in our story. This fluidity is, in my opinion, part of the fascination of late medieval Japan and indeed of other periods of globalization.

The supposedly Eurocentric nature of the Christian Century is doubly fraught due to its Iberian focus. Traditional views of early modern Europe trace the spread of "progress" from the Renaissance south to the Protestant north—where the true roots of modern capitalism lay. Japan's acceptance of Iberian Catholicism thus appeared superstitious and anti-modern. However, recent research has critiqued the emphasis on the northern or Atlantic emergence of modernity, exploring Iberian, Southeast Asian and other networks of circulation. Sixteenth-century European traders in East Asia were already riding on the back of the Chinese medieval economic revolution, which had led to the Japanese economy becoming increasingly commercialized. In the sixteenth century that commercialization became supercharged through the combination of warlords who needed to finance military campaigns and Iberian merchants who offered new opportunities for trade. Europeans reached Japanese waters at a time of instability and power vacuums often filled by maritime pirates. The term used in Japan for Europeans—*namban* or "Southern Barbarian"—had previously been applied to a range of peoples from the south, including raiders from the Ryukyu Islands. In the sixteenth century, *namban* linked the new arrivals with the Indian Ocean. Iberian merchants and missionaries both exploited the liminal, multi-ethnic spaces of sixteenth-century maritime East Asia. In Japan they invariably used the pirate ports of Kyushu.[7] This background helps explain both the success and limits of Iberian power in Japan. The limits were quickly recognized by Alessandro Valignano (1539–1606), Visitor for Jesuit activities east of Africa, who reported that "Japan is not a place which can be controlled by foreigners, for the Japanese are neither so weak nor so stupid a race as to permit this, and the King of Spain neither had nor ever could have any power of jurisdiction here."

---

**7** Erik Glowark, "The Christian Seas of Kyushu: How Local Maritime Networks Facilitated the Introduction of Catholicism to Japan in the Mid-Sixteenth Century," *Journal of World History* 33 (2022): 233–64.

The second historiographic problem with the Christian Century relates to periodization. 1600 marks the division between medieval and early modern in Japan, a distinction borrowed from Europe in the early twentieth century in an attempt to emphasize the universal, hence "civilized" aspects of the Japanese past. While there continues to be considerable discussion over how best to characterize these periods, the division itself has become ingrained in Japanese scholarship. The Christian Century not only inconveniently straddles the two periods, its central motif seems to have little explanatory power regarding the transition between them. While this book explores the Christian Century as a time of dynamic change, existing periodizations in Japanese history emphasize stability over the same period. The time from 1467, the start of the Ōnin War, to 1568, when warlord Oda Nobunaga (1534–1582) occupied Kyoto, is known as the Warring States, a label borrowed from early Chinese history. The years from 1568 to 1582, when Nobunaga died after an ambush by one of his generals, are then called the *Azuchi* period, after Nobunaga's castle on Lake Biwa. The following stage, lasting until the unification of the *daimyō* barons in 1598 by Toyotomi Hideyoshi (1536–1598) is termed *Momoyama*, referring to Hideyoshi's castle located between Kyoto and Osaka. Both Azuchi and Momoyama are named after élite buildings, reflecting the growing power of the warlords who were unifying Japan but side-lining a broader global history into a narrative of national unification.

This book follows my recent research in attempting to place Japanese history in a Eurasian or global context. In trying to see Japan "on its own terms," we often miss the bigger picture. For some observers, globalization implies a one-way street of incorporation into a homogenous culture. My work on the Bronze Age has shown how globalization also leads to tension and resistance, and it is such processes that I find of interest. I use the term Christian Century to refer to a period of dynamic contact between Eurasian and American societies in the Japanese Islands from 1543 to 1639. At times this simply serves as a convenient shorthand for "Japan in the second half of the sixteenth and the first four decades of the seven-teenth century." Given the role played by merchants, there is an argument for abandoning the label "Christian." Antonio Cabezas's important book *El Siglo Ibérico de Japón* suggests one alternative, the "European Century" might be another. Brett Walker has proposed "Japan's global century." Other historians have written about Japan's "long sixteenth cen-tury," emphasizing the persistence of medieval structures to the end of our period. While this perspective may resonate within Japanese historiography, Japan's sixteenth-century global encounter was with societies that were early modern. With respect to the label "Christian," there is no question that Jesuit and mendicant missions played a pivotal role. Canon law forbade clerics from engaging in trade but in Japan the Society of Jesus obtained a special dispensation from Rome for participation in the silk trade. Jesuits were even involved in the Portuguese slave trade in Japan. In the 1580s, Luis de Guzmán noted how the Jesuit compound in Nagasaki resem-bled the Customs House of Seville with its newly arrived mer-chandise, including slaves.[8]

The Christian Century parallels a dynamic period in Euro-pean history between the Reformation and the Thirty Years War. The Catholic Counter-Reformation forms a key backdrop to our story. As Catholicism began its resurgence, Christian-ity became the first global religion and Japan was seen as a harbinger of great expectations for a reformed Church. A highly civilized nation open to debate and conversion through reason, in the words of Francis Xavier the Japanese were "the best people yet discovered." If Japan was initially the most successful Catholic mission in Asia, however, that success was short-lived. By 1639 Christianity was outlawed and Ibe-rian traders had been replaced by the Dutch. Yet, in ways we shall explore, the Iberian influence on Japan was far-reaching. This calls for some explanation. Across Asia, early modern

---

**8** Some individual Jesuits opposed the slave trade. See also Kōichirō Takase, "Unauthorized Commercial Activities by Jesuit Missionaries in Japan," *Acta Asiatica* 30 (1976): 19–33.

European settlement was limited to small coastal enclaves. Europe had little that Asians wanted to buy, except the silver they shipped from South America and Japan. In terms of population, the European kingdoms involved in the Christian Century were small. Wayne Farris estimates the population of Japan in 1600 at between fifteen and seventeen million. The lower end of this range is equivalent to the *combined* populations of Portugal, Spain, the Dutch Republic, and England and Wales at the same time. While historians have long puzzled over Spain's "improbable empire," there are several interesting points of similarity between the transition from medieval to early modern in Iberia and Japan, including popular religiosity, exile and exclusion, urbanization, and violence and the expansion of state power.[9]

This book explores the end of medieval Japan from three perspectives: religion, violence, and exchange. Chapter 2 looks at the remarkable spread of Christianity. The combination of numerous conversions followed quickly by persecution gave Japan a special place in the Catholic imaginary. On the Japanese side, our Century was marked by the violent imposition of religious orthodoxies following the spread of popular schools of Buddhism in the medieval era. Chapter 3 considers violence and state-building. The Tokugawa instituted a bureaucratic state that unified the nation after the chaos of the late Middle Ages. Charles Tilly and others have argued that warfare was a key factor in state formation and the chapter examines the role of violence in the establishment of Tokugawa hegemony. Chapter 4 looks at economic and cultural exchange between Japan and the wider world. American crops such as sweet potato, chilli peppers and tobacco began to be cultivated in Japan. Iberian dietary customs, including the use of eggs in new recipes, influenced Japanese cuisine.

---

**9** Felipe Fernández-Armesto, "The Improbable Empire," in *Spain: A History*, ed. Raymond Carr (Oxford: Oxford University Press, 2000), 116–51; Bartolomé Yun-Casalilla, *Iberian World Empires and the Globalization of Europe, 1415–1668* (Singapore: Palgrave Macmillan, 2019).

New trading connections also brought treponemal disease to Japan, perhaps for the first time. Syphilis spread rapidly, affecting a large proportion of the population. The encounter with Europe encouraged transcultural expressions wherein even non-Christian Japanese wore rosaries and crucifixes as fashion items. Chapter 5 attempts some conclusions on the interplay between the global and the local in the century of transition between medieval and early modern Japan.

Chapter 2

# "The Best People Yet Discovered": Japan and the Counter-Reformation

While there had probably been some earlier knowledge of Nestorian or other forms of Christianity in Japan, the sixteenth century marked a dramatic new religious encounter. The Iberian missions to Japan were an important vanguard of the Catholic Counter-Reformation and the formation of the first global religion. At a time when, from the Catholic perspective, Christendom seemed under threat as never before, Japan offered hope of new conversions, albeit achieved through accommodation to a very different civilization. The Jesuits in particular approached conversion from a broad political and intellectual standpoint, learning the language and cultural mores of Japan and cultivating close relations with the élites.

Medieval Japan was marked by the growing influence of popular Buddhist sects, a trend which, in certain respects, set the scene for the later acceptance of Christianity. The most radical challenge came from the monk Hōnen (1133–1212) who, like Luther more than three centuries later, argued that religion should be a matter of individual practice without relying on the intermission of priests or mediatory gods and saints. Chanting the name of the Amida Buddha made salvation available to anyone regardless of social status. Hōnen's True Pure Land (*Jōdo Shinshū*) movement was opposed by Nichiren (1222–1282), a monk whose Lotus Sutra sect assigned a greater role to traditional structures of social authority. Within Japanese Buddhism, the True Pure Land

and especially Nichiren movements developed exclusivist tendencies. True Pure Land became known as the *ikkō* or "Singled-Minded" school. Violent insurgencies by this group included a 1532 attack on Kōfukuji temple in Nara when sutras and other religious objects were burnt. From 1532–1536, Lotus Sect leagues took over Kyoto before they were slaughtered by a religious-warrior coalition based on the Tendai school Enryakuji temple.

Despite doctrinal differences, the True Pure Land and Lotus movements were both centred on towns and merchant networks. Yoshihiko Amino called them "mercantilist religions," a framing which could include Christianity. In Amino's reading, the success of these mercantilist religions was such that the barons who attempted to unify Japan on the basis of "agrarian fundamentalism" were forced into violent conflict with their adherents. As early as 1570, Nobunaga launched a siege of Osaka, the True Pure Land headquarters, although he only managed to capture the city a decade later. In 1574, Nobunaga used several hundred ships with cannon to destroy True Pure Land bases in Ise province, killing some twenty thousand followers. Nobunaga's persecution of Buddhism helped the Christian missionaries in several ways, including the availability of buildings for purchase. In 1577, Jesuit Luís Fróis (1532–1597) explained that "The reason why these monks sell their temples and monasteries where they live is because the King Nobunaga is gradually destroying and taking away their property...The monks sell what they have in order to get funds to live." Why the mercantilist religions were not able to maintain independent power bases and how the vibrant mercantile and maritime tradition of early Japan became dominated by land-based agrarianism after 1600 may, Amino muses, "be the most important issue in the overall history of Japanese society."[1]

Like so many other aspects of Japanese history, the flowering and persecution of medieval Buddhism has been

---

[1] Yoshihiko Amino, *Rethinking Japanese History* (Ann Arbor: Center for Japanese Studies, University of Michigan, 2012), 168.

interpreted in terms of the goal posts of modernity. Griffis portrayed Buddhism as antithetical to modernization, using language evoking the Catholic church prior to the Reformation. Buddhism, he decried, had "degenerated into a commercial system of prayers and masses, in which salvation could be purchased only by the merit, of the deeds and prayers of the priests." It nevertheless retained its outward splendour and it was the comparable ritualistic elements of Catholicism that appealed to the Japanese: "The priests of Rome came with crucifixes in their hands, eloquence on their lips, and with rich dresses, impressive ceremonies, processions, and mysteries out-dazzled the scenic displays of the Buddhists." Outward similarities eased the transition between the faiths: statues of the Buddha or his saints could be transformed into Christian figures "after a little alteration with the chisel," the Cross replaced the *torii*, the Kannon Goddess of Mercy served as the Virgin Mary, and so on. In fact, Griffis insisted, "Almost every thing that is distinctive in the Roman form of Christianity is to be found in Buddhism," although his following list of thirty-seven offending items (plus three *et ceteras*) reflects an intensely Calvinist view of the faith.[2]

Other historians have approached medieval Buddhism as a more progressive phenomenon. In the late nineteenth century, Japanese scholars had called the Kamakura period (1185–1333) the time of Japan's "Buddhist Reformation." Despite some merit in this comparison it never took off, largely because it seemed so clearly *not* to connect to modernization in the way Weber had proposed for the Protestant Reformation in Europe.[3] While it is not my intention to resurrect this approach to Buddhism here, the underlying themes

---

**2** Griffis, *Mikado's Empire*, 272–73. The *torii* is a Shintō not a Buddhist structure.

**3** Robert Bellah, a scholar who wrote about the religious aspects of Japan's modernization, played down the importance of the "Buddhist Reformation" in "The Contemporary Meaning of Kamakura Buddhism," *Journal of the American Academy of Religion* 42 (1974): 3–17.

of religious diversity followed by new orthodoxies are relevant to our overall topic.

## The Catholic Mission in Japan

In 1549 Francis Xavier and two other Jesuits, together with two Japanese converts and three servants, reached Kagoshima from India. Several immediate problems faced Xavier and his party. One was the endemic warfare plaguing the country. Valignano later wrote how "Japan is never a firm whole, but is always revolving like a wheel." This instability brought both disadvantages and advantages for the Society of Jesus. The second problem was language. Although one member of Xavier's party had begun to learn Japanese on the boat from India, the group initially relied on Anjirō (a name also read Yajirō), a samurai from Kagoshima who had been baptized in Goa in 1548. Anjirō and Xavier translated the catechism used to propagate Christianity in Japan. Debate over this text arose as early as 1555 when Balthazar Gago (1515–1583) complained that it contained over fifty terms detrimental to a true understanding of the faith. The major point of contention was the use of Buddhist terminology, especially the translation of God as *Dainichi*, a word used for the Mahāvairocana "Great Sun," the main deity of Shingon Buddhism. In Yamaguchi in 1551, Xavier was surprised to encounter Shingon priests who thought he was propagating a version of the same teaching. At that point, Xavier stopped using *Dainichi* and adopted the Latin *Deus* instead (although this word was not without problems since it sounded similar to Japanese *dai-uso* or "great lie").

The question of translation reflected broader issues of inter-cultural communication. Anjirō had attended a Jesuit college in Goa and probably had a better doctrinal understanding of Christianity than Buddhism. It is unclear if Anjirō's claim that the Japanese believed in "only one God, the creator of all things" was an attempt to ingratiate himself with his Iberian protectors or reflected his understanding of Shingon Buddhism. In 1548, Nicolò Lancilotto made three reports on religion in Japan based on information from Anjirō. The latter's explanation of Buddhism in Christian terms encouraged Lancilotto to speculate about earlier contact between Japan and Christianity. At the time this was a common though self-reinforcing belief. Fróis wrote that the Japanese "are learning Christian customs so naturally that sometimes it even appears to me that these people have been Christians from the old days." Back in Europe, this theme was taken up by French Orientalist and polymath Guillaume Postel (1510–1581) in support of an original universalist religion.[4]

If theological parallels seemed suggestive, Japan's very different culture was a major challenge. From Kyushu, Xavier travelled to the capital of Kyoto, a city in ruins due to war, a "lair of wolves and foxes." In part due to his pauper-like appearance, Xavier was unable to gain an audience with the emperor or to enter a Buddhist monastery on Mount Hiei, part of one of the most important temple complexes in the country. The need to dress in a way appropriate to local norms would also become an issue in China where Jesuit Matteo Ricci (1552-1610) grew his hair and beard and wore the robes of a Confucian *literatus*. East Asian cultures forced a re-imagining of missionary work in a very different way from the encounter with Native America. For some Jesuits Japan suggested a parallel with the early propagation of Christianity to pagan Greece and Rome. Valignano's letters spoke of Japan as a new "primitive Church." If Protestantism afforded believers a chance to return to a more genuine Christianity based directly on the Bible, Japan seemed to offer an equally "authentic" context resembling the early Church. For this reason, Antoni Uceler argues that the Catholic mission in Japan encouraged nothing less than a re-invention of the faith.

By the late sixteenth century the Society of Jesus possessed a powerful global network. Japan was the largest Jesuit enterprise east of Goa and the only place in Asia where

---

**4** Jeff Persels, "A Curious Case of Ethnographic Cleansing: The First French Interpretations of the Japanese, 1552–1555," *L'esprit créateur* 48 (2008): 45–57.

the Society asked for a monopoly on their work. Pope Gregory XIII entrusted the Japanese mission exclusively to the Jesuits in 1585, though this was rescinded in 1600. Japan had many attractions for the Society and the Counter-Reformation more generally. Valignano concluded that "Japan is, without a doubt, the most important and fruitful enterprise that has been undertaken in the lands of the East Indies." The people "are white, very civilized, prudent, intelligent and subject to reason." Naturally religious, "Of all the peoples in the Orient, only the Japanese are moved to become Christians by their own free will." The situation in Japan contrasted with, and to an extent made up for, a troubled Europe where Protestantism was extending its influence. Catholic printer Johann Mayer exclaimed in 1585 that "in the place of so many thousand souls in Upper and Lower Germany" who were tempted by the "Evil Enemy," God had elected another people from the other side of the world. It was also noticed that, just as one island nation at the western edge of Eurasia had been lost to the true faith, another island off the eastern edge seemed ripe for conversion. Gaspar Gonçalves made this connection between England and Japan during a 1585 papal audience for three Japanese Christians. As the Spanish Armada prepared to leave port, Pedro Ribadeñeira preached that the conversion of Japan provided a model for retaking England.

As mentioned, Jesuit leaders realized the impossibility of European rule over Japan. Accommodation to Japanese culture was emphasized by Valignano who, upon his arrival in Japan, criticized mission leader Francisco Cabral (1533–1609) who looked down on the Japanese and their customs. Cabral was relieved of his post and schools were established to educate both sides: a novitiate in Usuki, a college in Funai, and two preparatory schools in Arima. Under Valignano's direction, Jesuits in Japan sometimes wore the robes of Buddhist priests. Furthermore, the faith would have to be propagated by native priests, an approach unknown elsewhere. In order to convince the Church that the Japanese were up to this task, Valignano sent four teenage converts to Rome in 1582. These boys became "actors in a conversion drama orchestrated by the Jesuits to impress Europe's Catholic elite and to secure their support of the Jesuit enterprise in Japan."[5] It seems likely that the *Tratado*, the treatise on Japanese culture attributed to Fróis, resulted from the same strategy. In a striking example of proto-anthropological cultural relativism, Fróis explained that the Japanese were different—in fact, *very* different—but still highly civilized. The *Tratado* is all the more remarkable because Fróis had left his native Portugal at age sixteen, never to return to Europe.

Jesuit efforts quickly bore fruit. The number of Christian churches in Japan grew from nine in 1560, to forty in 1569, and around two hundred by 1583. By the 1570s, some 100,000 Japanese had been baptized. A maximum of 300,000 converts is widely cited. Fernão Gurreiro reported 750,000 Christians in 1605, a figure which excludes the smaller number of converts made by the mendicant orders.[6] While Boxer finds Gurreiro's claim exaggerated, there is no doubt that a very large number of Japanese were influenced by Christianity in some way, whether or not they were formally baptized. The conversions were made by a small number of clerics, the maximum being reached in 1614 with 137 foreign and seven Japanese priests. In many cases feudal barons played a key role, their baptisms leading to thousands of converts in their territories. Such cases are sometimes presented as evidence that most Japanese had to be coerced into accepting a foreign religion. Yet many parts of Reformation Europe saw similar princely conversions. The motto summing up the 1555 Peace of Augsburg—*cuius regio, eius religio* ("the prince's religion in the prince's lands")—can also be applied to Japan.

---

**5** Daniel Reff, "Critical Introduction: The *Tratado*, the Jesuits, and the Governance of Souls," in *The First European Description of Japan*, 15. Where a short-form citation is provided at the first reference to a source, please consult the Further Reading at the end for further details.

**6** Boxer suggested a figure of a few thousand for the latter category, but Takeshi Gonoi argued that the Franciscans acquired more than 26,000 converts in the Tōhoku region between 1614 and 1629.

Figure 2.1 *Miyako no nambandera* ("Southern Barbarian Temple
in Kyoto"). Fan painting, ca. 1578–1587.
Courtesy of Kobe City Museum.

Conversions were further encouraged by care for the sick and poor, not least by Christian lay confraternities. In Nagasaki, the Misericórdia brotherhood counted more than a hundred citizens among its members and gave food, clothing, and medicine to widows, orphans, and the destitute. Mihoko Oka writes that "The efforts of the missionaries to save the sick and poor attracted the scorn of the Japanese; at the same time … for those Japanese who lived in the Warring States (*Sengoku*) period and for whom tomorrow was uncertain, the act of serving others must have seemed a fresh idea."[7]

Early Christian church buildings in Japan are poorly known since they were all destroyed in the seventeenth century. Many were abandoned Buddhist temples. Following local tradition, wood and other materials were frequently re-used for church construction. Archaeological excavations at the Santo Domingo church in Nagasaki have been combined with documentary sources to reconstruct the floor plan. A contem-

---

**7** Mihoko Oka, "The Catholic Missionaries and the Unified Regime in Japan," in *Palgrave Handbook of the Catholic Church in East Asia*, ed. C. Y. Chu and B. Leung (Singapore: Palgrave Macmillan, 2021), 1–35, here 7.

porary illustration of a church by Kanō Sōshū is thought to depict *Our Lady of the Assumption* in Kyoto, consecrated in 1578 and destroyed in 1587 (Figure 2.1). This unusual church had three floors in a neighbourhood where other buildings were single-storey, likely in an attempt to impress the local inhabitants.

While a small village had existed there before, Nagasaki was established as a town by the Jesuits in 1571 and became the physical centre of Japan's Christian Century. Nagasaki had perhaps the best natural harbour in Kyushu. Until 1614, virtually all permanent inhabitants of the town were baptized Christians. By 1600, Nagasaki was the fifth largest city in Japan with around 15,000 inhabitants, a number that grew to over 25,000 by 1613, making it the largest Christian town in Asia at the time. Attacks on Nagasaki by neighbouring barons necessitated a defensive wooden palisade, later replaced by a stone wall, although the precise nature of these fortifications is unclear.

## Christian Cemeteries

Archaeological research on early Christian burials in Japan has a history of more than a century. Recent excavations have vastly increased the corpus of such graves.[8] Early modern Japan was characterized by a great diversity of burial styles, though square or circular pits with bodies placed in wooden tubs in a sitting position was a common Buddhist style. Christian graves are distinguished above all by rectangular pits and an extended, supine positioning of the corpse. The body is sometimes, though not always, buried facing east. Many of the earliest Christian cemeteries in Japan were built on flat ground. In northwest Kyushu this marked a clear contrast with Buddhist cemeteries constructed at the base of mountains. Japanese archaeologists argue this reflects

---

**8** This section draws on Yoshitaka Kobayashi et al., eds., *Kirishitan haka kenkyū to kōkogaku*, special issue of *Kikan Kōkogaku* no. 164 (2023).

an attempt to bring the community of believers together in death, as opposed to the traditional Japanese practice of burial by family unit. Christian cemeteries are known from all over Japan from Kyushu to the Tohoku.

A 2012 publication listed 192 Christian gravestones from early modern Japan, the majority (76%) from Nagasaki prefecture. Gravestones could be inscribed with the name and date of death of the deceased, a cross, or with Christograms such as IHS, the emblem of the Society of Jesus. The earliest dated gravestone is from 1581 from Osaka. Grave goods are an important though infrequent find from Christian burials. The Takatsukijō cemetery in Osaka had twenty-seven Christian graves but only two produced grave goods, a proportion typical of other sites. Medals, rosary beads and crucifixes are the most common finds. Devotional medals, which became common in Catholic Europe from the sixteenth century, tie Japan to the global Counter-Reformation. An especially important aspect of archaeological research on Christian burials in Japan has been the discovery that Christian influence on mortuary customs continued long *after* the prohibition of the religion by the Tokugawa regime. The use of extended burials in rectangular pits and grave goods such as medals were associated with burials of the crypto-Christians discussed below.

Archaeologists have applied new scientific methods to several Christian grave sites. At Sendaiji, a site in Osaka with burials of both Buddhist and Christian villagers, stable isotope analysis found no significant dietary differences between the two groups. Stable isotopes and DNA were used to investigate remains possibly belonging to William Adams, and DNA has supported the identification of the grave of Giovanni Sidoti (1668-1714), an Italian missionary who entered Japan after the ban on Christianity. Anthropologists even made a facial reconstruction of Sidoti from his skull.[9]

**9** Takuya Tsutaya, Minoru Yoneda, Mikiko Abe, and Tomohito Nagaoka, "Carbon, Nitrogen, and Sulfur Stable Isotopic Reconstruction of Human Diet in a Mountainous Woodland Village in Sendaiji in Pre-

## The Sephardic Century

The Christian Century was also a *converso* century. A number of Iberian Jews who had been forced to convert to Catholicism are found among the traders and missionaries in Japan. Ignatius of Loyola supported the recruitment of *conversos* into the Society of Jesus against the opposition of many members (including Xavier). After Loyola's death, this recruitment was banned in 1593, with previously admitted Jesuits often forced to work outside Europe. One such individual was Pedro Gómez (1533–1600), who became head of the mission in Japan in 1590. Another important *converso* was Portuguese merchant and surgeon Luís de Almeida (1525–1583) who donated his fortune to the Jesuits after entering the Society at Funai in 1556. Almeida worked tirelessly in the medical field, as did Aires Sanches who was admitted to the Society in 1562 and became proficient in Japanese prior to his death in Kyushu in 1590.

The *converso* community in Nagasaki often faced disapproval from Japanese Christians. Their consumption of meat on Fridays and Saturdays was particularly shocking. Rui Pérez and his sons were chased through the streets and called "Jews." Faced with impending arrest by the Head Captain of Macau in 1591, Pérez escaped to Manila under Jesuit protection. In the Philippines, Pérez continued his business in counterfeit religious relics until he was denounced to the Inquisition in 1597 and sent to Mexico, dying two days before arrival.[10]

---

modern Japan," *Anthropological Science* 127 (2019): 131–38; Fuzuki Mizuno, Koji Ishiya, Masami Matsushita, Takayuki Matsushita, Katherine Hampson, Michiko Hayashi, Fuyuki Tokanai, Kunihiko Kurosaki, and Shintaroh Ueda, "A Biomolecular Anthropological Investigation of William Adams, the First SAMURAI from England," *Scientific Reports* 10 (2020): e21651; Etsuo Ikeda, "Senkyōshi Sidoti no haka," *Kikan Kōkogaku* 164 (2023): 45–50.

**10** Lúcio de Sousa, "The Jewish Presence in China and Japan in the Early Modern Period: A Social Representation," in *Global History and New Polycentric Approaches: Europe, Asia and the Americas in*

Against the background of this *converso* presence, an underground room at Hitoyoshi castle in central Kyushu is of considerable interest. A 6 by 5.2 metre stone chamber has a 2.3-metre-deep pool with steps, fed by a natural spring. Thought to have been destroyed in 1640, the room was constructed in the late sixteenth or early seventeenth centuries based on excavated ceramics. The room appears remarkably similar to a *mikveh* used for Jewish ablutions. Alternatively, some historians have suggested it was employed in Buddhist purification ceremonies, but in that case it is unclear why the room was hidden underground and why there are no similar examples found elsewhere. The *mikveh* theory faces equally difficult questions about the presence of Jewish practices in seventeenth-century Hitoyoshi.[11]

## Christianity and 'Folk Religion'

Japanese historians stress that the reception of Christianity in sixteenth-century Japan was filtered through native religious practices and therefore differed fundamentally from Europe. Japan, insists Ikuo Higashibaba, did not produce "full-fledged European-style Christians." Terms like "convert" and "Christian" are, he argues, misleading because they imply a uniformity of belief. The most radical view of the Christian

---

*a World Network System*, ed. Manuel P. Garcia and Lúcio de Sousa (Singapore: Palgrave Macmillan, 2018), 183–218, and Lúcio de Sousa, *The Portuguese Slave Trade*, 313–27. The production of fake historical objects was a strategy also used by *moriscos* to gain equality with Old Christians: see Margarita Diaz-Andreu, "Archaeology and Nationalism in Spain," in *Nationalism, Politics and the Practice of Archaeology*, ed. Philip Kohl and Clare Fawcett (Cambridge: Cambridge University Press, 1995), 39–56.

11 Excavations are reported in *Hitoyoshijō-ato X*, ed. Hitoyoshi Board of Education (Hitoyoshi: Hitoyoshi City, 1999). A photo of the room and discussion of various theories about its function appeared in "Experts Baffled by Mystery of Old Bathing Facility in Castle Ruins", *Asahi Shimbun*. www.asahi.com/ajw/articles/14775576, accessed July 12, 2024.

Century is one that denies the existence of Christianity in Japan. Instead, it is suggested, there was a unique religion whose practitioners can be called *Kirishitan* (a word derived from Portuguese *Christão*). This proposal was first made in the 1950s with respect to later crypto-Christians, but has recently been extended to the Century itself. Oka insists that "the Christianity prevalent in Japan during this period should not be regarded as true "Christianity" but as a unique Japanese religion called 'Kirishitan.'"[12]

These claims need to be understood against the extraordinary valorization of the "folk" in modern Japan. Influential scholars such as Kunio Yanagita (1875–1962) and Shinobu Orikuchi (1887–1953) developed a folkloristics or "native ethnology" which searched for "original," pre-capitalist social forms to re-contextualize or even challenge the deep changes experienced by Japan under modernity. The idea of a "folk religion"—which retained the enduring power of a Japanese tradition impervious to modernity and secularism—took on a new significance. Ichirō Hori's *Folk Religion in Japan* (1974) saw Christianity as an extreme yet representative example of how the Japanese "little tradition" incorporates outside religious elements. Higashibaba follows the same approach, claiming that Japan's "overall symbolic system, viz. religious system" remained "intact" despite the impact of Christianity.

In these debates, the Japanese "folk" is used to calibrate or deflect outside influences on religion in Japan without any acknowledgement of popular religious beliefs in Europe. Despite great transformations in the sixteenth and seven-

---

12 Ikuo Higashibaba, *Christianity in Early Modern Japan: Kirishitan Belief and Practice* (Leiden: Brill, 2001), xv; Oka, *The Namban Trade*, 1. The word *Kirishitan* is problematic because from the mid-seventeenth century it began to be used for a broader category of "deviancy" against the state: see Jan Leuchtenberger, *Conquering Demons: The "Kirishitan," Japan, and the World in Early-Modern Japanese Literature* (Ann Arbor: Center for Japanese Studies, University of Michigan, 2013).

teenth centuries, popular religious practices remained fundamental to European society. Felipe Fernández-Armesto emphasizes popular rituals and mysticism at the time of Spain's early empire, muddying the waters of what might be meant by concepts like "full-fledged European-style Christians."[13] Popular practices across Europe in the Reformation period included festivals, pilgrimages, cults of saints, blessing of Easter eggs, amulets and traditional healing, rural shrines and crosses, beliefs in fairies, sacred trees, and springs, and even the excommunication of rats, locusts, and other agricultural pests. There was no simple confessional divide. Protestants sometimes banned practices that Catholic reformers attempted to maintain in a more measured fashion. In 1616, the Catholic bishop of Speyer banned masks and actors in the carnival (*Fastnacht*) but insisted he did not wish to "forbid honourable meetings and moderate drinking against thirst"; this was in contrast to neighbouring Protestant communities where *Fastnacht* had been banned half a century earlier. In the Pays de Vaud, seventeenth-century villagers venerated a sacred tree trunk they believed could cure gout. In Untergrombach north of Karlsruhe, a traditional cure involved reciting a sacrilegious prayer while walking naked around the church altar. The *Weiberfastnacht* women's carnival held on Ash Wednesday was another custom that shocked Catholic reformers. On this night, women drank heavily as they symbolically took over the village and chased after men. While denouncing such "pagan" customs, Jesuits in the Upper Palatinate had no compunction about distributing "Xavier water" which had supposedly been in contact with a relic of the famous missionary. As late as the eighteenth century, peasants in the Eifel applied this holy water to their fields to eliminate a plague of caterpillars.[14] These examples will seem

---

13 Fernández-Armesto, "The Improbable Empire."

14 Marc Forster, *The Counter-Reformation in the Villages: Religion and Reform in the Bishopric of Speyer, 1560–1720* (Ithaca: Cornell University Press, 1992), 99, 236; Peter Marshall, *The Reformation: A Very Short Introduction* (Oxford: Oxford University Press, 2009), 91.

unremarkable to European historians but are worth repeating to contextualize the Japanese situation.

Stephen Turnbull proposes that some folk practices found in Japanese Christianity were transmitted directly from sixteenth-century Europe. Counter-Reformation edicts in Europe were often hostile to wooden crosses erected in the countryside, yet Jesuits in Japan made widespread use of such landmarks. Hundreds of people would gather to receive relics and Japanese Christians of all social classes embraced self-flagellation. In 1563 it was recorded from Ikitsuki that "as night set in, prior to receiving the Eucharist at midnight, [believers] whipped their bodies fervently in front of crosses in the church or in the surrounding forest." Flagellant processions recalled those in Europe although, outside of Italy and Spain, self-flagellation was seen as a public nuisance and was repeatedly banned in Bavaria in the eighteenth century. Japanese believers also wore crowns of thorns and bore crosses during Good Friday re-enactments. Turnbull further analyzes how the *Tenchi hajimari no koto* ("Concerning the Creation of Heaven of Earth"), a crypto-Christian work transmitted orally until being committed to writing in the 1820s, contains apocryphal and non-canonical material showing the Jesuits must have included such "folk" elements in their proselytization.[15]

Higashibaba counters that Turnbull's thesis is only partially applicable because Japanese converts could choose aspects of Christianity that they found of value and combine them with existing practices. As a result, "Japanese followers' eclectic religious practice...[was] remarkably unique and essentially different from popular practice in Europe that had long been dominated by Christianity." Such comments privilege existing religious practice in Japan, but it should be remembered that Japanese believers were actively incorporating aspects of a completely *new* religion. Jesuits could also

---

15 Stephen Turnbull, "Acculturation among the *Kakure Kirishitan*: Some Conclusions from the *Tenchi hajimari no koto*," in *Japan and Christianity: Impacts and Responses*, ed. John Breen and Mark Williams (Basingstoke: Macmillan, 1996), 63–74.

be open to Japanese folk practice. Trees provide an interesting example. Guillaume Alonge has discussed how growing persecutions led to a shift from wooden crosses placed prominently in the landscape to holy trees, often with thaumaturgical properties. As man-made crosses were cut down by the authorities, natural crosses were discovered inside or on the trunks of trees in the forest. Wood from these trees became associated with miracles, attracting Japanese who understood the overlap with native beliefs.

The power and persistence of popular beliefs were clear to the Catholic Church. Rural areas of Spain were compared to "the Indies" as priests tried to instruct people who, they complained, were ignorant of basic features of the faith. In Japan, points of contact between Christian and local traditions became subject to theological debate. In 1593 Pedro Gómez explained in great detail the behaviour acceptable for converts under the rule of non-Christian lords. Japanese believers had inquired about the Obon Buddhist All Souls Festival, the Gion festival in Kyoto, and the display of decorative pine branches (*kadomatsu*) at New Year. These were allowed, Gómez concluded, as long as it was understood that no religious benefits would accrue: "To perform dances is not forbidden at all. [But] to light lanterns and to offer sake and rice in the belief that the spirits will return is futile. If your lord strongly insists that you light a lantern, you should not hesitate to do it; but pretend you do not know [what it is for]." The responses made by Gómez and other Jesuits show that the accommodation of Christianity to Japan reflected local folk practices.

Marriage was one area where popular practice took on wider significance. In Europe, clerical concubinage, a common custom in the Middle Ages, came into direct conflict with Tridentine reforms. In Lyon, episcopal visitors found that seventeen per cent of priests had concubines in the late fourteenth century. In Speyer in the 1580s, more than half of priests were found to be living with women, often the mothers of their children. The custom was usually accepted by parishioners, except where the priest had two or more women or mistreated them. Financial considerations were invoked to support concubinage; priests complained their incomes were insufficient to keep servants, unless (by implication) household help was provided by someone who did not require a salary.[16] In Japan, Valignano argued that it would be impossible to introduce even the ideal of Christian marriage found in Europe since the Japanese were always "switching estates and kingdoms" due to incessant warfare. They did not take their wives when "exiled," but "given the duties which the soldiers have, it is out of the question for them to live without wives, so wherever they go they marry again." Imposing a Christian doctrine of marriage, Valignano concluded, would be "an impediment and indeed a disaster as far as the propagation and acceptance of our holy law is concerned."[17] At times the Jesuits did, however, arrange marriages for prostitutes from impoverished families

An extension of the "folk" approach to late medieval/early modern Christianity in Japan is one which argues it was misunderstood as a type of Buddhism. Mihoko Oka, ever one for certainty over controversial issues, claims this link is "undeniable."[18] Oka bases her argument on four points. First, that the clothing and shaved heads of some missionaries recalled the appearance of Buddhist monks; second, that because European missionaries were so few, propagation of the faith relied on Japanese brothers (*iruman*, from Portuguese *irmão*) and assistants (*dojuku*) who naturally had a better knowledge of Buddhism; third, that Jesuit accommodation to Japanese

---

**16** Philip Hoffman, *Church and Community in the Diocese of Lyon, 1500-1789* (New Haven: Yale University Press, 1984), 50; Forster, *Counter-Reformation in the Villages*, 22–26.

**17** On Church attitudes to marriage in Japan, see Luisa S. de Oliveira Coutinho Silva, "The Janus Face of Normativities in a Global Mirror: Viewing 16th-Century Marriage Practices in Japan from Christian and Japanese Traditions," in *Norms Beyond Empire: Law-making and Local Normativities in Iberian Asia, 1500-1800*, ed Manuel Bastias Saavedra (Leiden: Brill, 2021), 171–206.

**18** Oka, "The Catholic Missionaries and the Unified Regime."

cultural patterns encouraged overlap between the faiths; and fourth, that Japanese crypto-Christians felt a strong sense of incompatibility with the Catholic Church when they came out of hiding in the nineteenth century. I find none of these arguments to be convincing or supported by the evidence presented. Questions of dress and appearance were certainly of concern to the Jesuit fathers, who sometimes shifted between European and Japanese styles due to considerations of prestige and personal safety.[19] While this may have generated confusion at times, it would be an exaggeration to use this as proof of a fundamental misconstruction of Christianity. Oka's second and third points are not substantiated by any concrete evidence and rely on ideas about the mutual exclusion of "Eastern" and "Western" thought. As regards crypto-Christians, it is more likely that they rejected the racist views held by nineteenth-century Westerners. Oka's argument is further contradicted by her own comment that Nobunaga used Christianity *against* powerful Buddhist movements, instructing his retainers that "rather than killing many monks and destroying their temples, protect the missionaries and help to spread their teachings." The disputed issue of modernity is again part of the equation. Oka claims a "clear difference exists between modern Japanese, who have some knowledge of Christianity due to the positive acceptance and popularization of Western culture after the Meiji era, and those of the sixteenth and seventeenth centuries, who accepted Christianity without prior knowledge." In other words, Christianity was so intrinsically linked with modernity that nineteenth-century Japanese were predisposed to an understanding of that faith as part of their modern project. In

---

**19** Disguise as poor travelling monks was one mechanism employed in the early years of the Jesuit mission when warfare was common; see Linda Zampol D'Ortia, "Purple Silk and Black Cotton: Francisco Cabral and the Negotiation of Jesuit Attire in Japan (1570–73)," in *Exploring Jesuit Distinctiveness: Interdisciplinary Perspectives on Ways of Proceeding within the Society of Jesus*, ed. Robert Maryks, 137–55 (Leiden: Brill, 2016).

the sixteenth and seventeenth centuries, by contrast, Japan was still premodern and thus unable to understand or accept "Western" culture.

## Kakugyō in the Wilderness: Christianity and Mount Fuji

If the folk influenced Christianity in Japan, did Christianity also impact the folk? Beliefs surrounding Mount Fuji provide a suggestive example. Fuji had been venerated from ancient times and the medieval period saw the growing influence of *yamabushi* mountain ascetics, figures described in Luis de Guzmán's 1601 *Historia de las missiones*. In 1618, the Tokugawa government issued injunctions against *yamabushi* as part of a general crackdown on religious expressions it considered in opposition to its power. Nevertheless, a new religious movement centred on Mount Fuji was established by an ascetic known as Kakugyō (1541–1646). By the late eighteenth century, this movement became enormously popular in Edo (modern Tokyo) and surrounding regions. *Fujikō* confraternities undertook pilgrimages to the mountain and began to call for *yonaoshi* or "world renewal," a trend that alarmed Tokugawa officials.

A text describing Kakugyō's life, the *Go-taigyō no maki* ("Book of the Great Practice"), seems to have been written in the late eighteenth or early nineteenth century, yet contains older material. In his translation, Royall Tyler noted that "In a way, [Kakugyō's] teaching resembles a sort of Judeo-Christian monotheism nativized almost, but not quite, beyond all recognition. Whether or not so perilous an idea is even faintly plausible, however, is difficult to judge."[20] Kakugyō was born in Nagasaki and, as a youth, would have encountered the growing Iberian influence in Kyushu. According to the *Book of Great Practice*, Kakugyō left Nagasaki in his eighteenth year.

---

**20** Royall Tyler, "'The Book of the Great Practice': The Life of the Mt Fuji Ascetic Kakugyō Tōbutsu Ku (Introduction and Translation)," *Asian Folklore Studies* 52 (1993): 251–331, here 281.

If that chronology can be believed, it would place his departure just before Nagasaki became a predominantly Christian town. By the 1570s, Ōmura Bartolomeu, the Christian lord of Nagasaki, was forcing non-Christians to leave the town. Against this background, it may not be coincidence that several aspects of the *Book* suggest a knowledge—though not necessarily an acceptance—of Christianity.

Kakugyō's birth had a miraculous aspect. His father, a samurai unable to prevent the distress caused by incessant warfare, beseeched Heaven for seven days until his prayer was answered by a message from the Polestar announcing it would borrow his wife's womb so his wish might be fulfilled. The son born as a result was "a manifestation of the Sun, Moon, and the Divine Stars, and of [the Fuji deity] Sengen Dainichi and the Polestar." Miraculous births were not unknown in the Japanese tradition. The *Jōgu Shōtoku Taishi den hoketsu ki*, a ninth-century biography of Prince Shōtoku (a semi-legendary figure attributed to 574–622), related that his mother had a dream in which a golden priest appeared and asked to borrow her womb in order to save the world. Upon accepting this "annunciation," the mother gave birth to the prince at a stable door. In 1905, historian Kunitake Kume suggested this story may have been carried back to Japan through contacts with Nestorian communities in China. Shōtoku was later connected to Mount Fuji in the 1431 *Sangoku denki* which recounted how the prince flew on his horse to the summit of the mountain. Even Hideyoshi claimed, in a 1590 letter to the king of Korea, that he had been conceived when the wheel of the sun entered his mother's womb in a dream.

The *Book of Great Practice* describes how Kakugyō began a life of ascetic endeavour, travelling to eastern provinces and engaging in fasts while awaiting a spiritual sign. An "oracle" from the seventh-century ascetic En-no-Gyōja directed him to Hitoana cave at the base of Mount Fuji. Local villagers told Kakugyō he should not enter lest it bring disaster, but after seven days of prayer at the nearby Shiraito waterfalls, a "celestial child" appeared and led him to the cave. In pitch darkness, Kakugyō vowed to test the righteousness of his way by jumping inside; he later jumped into a deep ravine on Fuji but again miraculously suffered no injuries. These accounts of avoiding injury while leaping into the unknown have a certain similarity—perhaps coincidental—with the temptation of Christ in the desert. The *Book* also records episodes of fasting in wild areas and miraculous cures performed by Kakugyō. Two disciples started to follow Kakugyō after he cured one of leprosy and the other of being deaf and dumb.

Given its late date, the *Book of Great Practice* cannot be considered a text from the Christian Century; elements suggestive of Christian influence might have been added later. However, that raises the further question of the source of such ideas at a time when Christianity was officially outlawed in Japan. A link with Kakugyō's lifetime seems more parsimonious, though impossible to prove from available records. Kakugyō himself was not a Christian, but he and his followers may have used stories from Christianity—together with other Japanese religions—to develop a popular vision of world renewal through Mount Fuji. The broader point is that we cannot place Christianity in a separate silo and assume it had no influence on other aspects of early modern Japanese society. If, as many scholars have proposed, Japanese folk beliefs influenced Christianity, some influence in the opposite direction must also be a possibility.

## Conclusions

The Christian Century saw perhaps the most remarkable transformation in Japanese religious history. Never before had so many people embraced a new faith in such a short time. Reaching Japan in the sixth century, Buddhism had gradually gained influence among the aristocracy, becoming the main religion of state after two centuries. Yet Buddhism remained primarily an élite faith for half a millennium after its introduction. Of course, available texts prioritize accounts of aristocratic over peasant beliefs, but the spread of Buddhism in Japan was comparatively slow. Without the Tokugawa persecutions, Christianity would likely have expanded even further in Japan. Only in the nineteenth century did new religions such as Tenrikyō begin to exceed the rapid pace of conversions achieved by Iberian Catholicism. Despite persecution, thousands of Japanese Christians steadfastly maintained their faith in secret until the late nineteenth century.

Japanese historians attempt to circumscribe the influence of Christianity in the sixteenth and seventeenth centuries by emphasizing folk beliefs as a sort of firewall against globalization. If, as proposed by Jesuits at the time, the spread of Christianity in Japan could be imagined as having parallels with the early church in Greece and Rome, we might borrow Peter Brown's term *roughage* for the imaginative and intellectual contributions of pre-Christian roots. Japan's first encounter with Christianity involved similar roughage in the shape of existing beliefs and practices. Japanese historians have nevertheless insisted on an idealised image of a "well-bred" Christianity in danger of "contamination" (again Peter Brown). Higashibaba's "full-fledged European-style Christians," which he misses in Japan, are in fact difficult to find in Europe in our period.

Catholicism's remarkable success in Japan, followed immediately by harsh persecution, gave the country an important symbolic role in the Counter-Reformation. Both Japanese Christians and European priests at first attempted to weather the persecutions via clandestine support networks which have yet to receive full attention in the literature: Chapter 4 mentions a Portuguese Jesuit who travelled to Hokkaido disguised as a Japanese gold miner. After all priests had been expelled, Christianity continued underground. The success of Christianity in late medieval Japan complicates narratives over early European colonialism. Japan is perhaps the clearest example of the *limits* of that colonialism in Asia. Despite initial Iberian successes in intermediary trade, by the 1640s only a small contingent of Dutch merchants was allowed to operate from Dejima island in Nagasaki harbour. Subject to numerous restrictions, the Dutch were even forbidden from burying their dead in Japanese soil and had to dispose of deceased countrymen at sea. Nevertheless, Christianity and Iberian culture had a broad, cascading impact on Japanese society in the total absence of military interventions such as those employed in the Americas.

# Chapter 3

# Violence and State-Building in the Christian Century

At the end of the sixteenth century, after more than two centuries of war, Japan was unified under the Tokugawa dynasty. Historians have discussed the role of Christianity and European firearms in this process. A common conclusion is that while the contribution of the latter has been over-exaggerated, the threat from Christianity was real. In this chapter I make the opposite argument. Rapidly adopted and manufactured by the Japanese themselves, firearms and other military technologies played a key—though not deterministic—role in political unification; the military threat from Europe at this time was, by contrast, minimal. My point of departure here is that violence needs to be placed in a much broader, contextual framework than traditionally used to understand Japan's Christian Century. Violence had both local and global aspects. We will discuss, for example, how harsh persecutions of Christians from the 1590s appear to have radicalized communities in Nagasaki. At a global scale, Volume 3 of the *Cambridge World History of Violence* notes how Nagasaki was connected to a trading network that, amongst other impacts, inadvertently perpetuated the brutal treatment of workers at the Potosí silver mine in Bolivia.

In Japanese history the dominant narrative of the Christian Century period is the "unification" of the country. After a long span of chaos, the nation was finally brought together through the heroic efforts of the three great hegemons—Nobunaga, Hideyoshi, and Ieyasu. It is acknowledged that this was, at base, a rather violent process, but the result was the "peace dividend" of the *Pax Tokugawana*. In this narrative it is the Europeans—pictured by one American historian as "hundreds of gun- and Bible-bearing Westerners who had come to make a profit and save souls"—who were the major menace to Japan's stability.[1] The West as threat underpins L. M. Cullen's *A History of Japan, 1582–1941* (2003), a book structured around a chronology during which Japan countered outside dangers. In Cullen's reading, Japan possessed a remarkable ability to meet such threats on her own terms, largely due to inherent cultural characteristics. Compared to the grim cruelties of Renaissance Europe, it has been suggested that the Japanese were enlightened and tolerant; even Hideyoshi is admired in this respect by Sansom. Given a Europe troubled by the Inquisition, religious wars and the slave trade, Sansom writes, Hideyoshi "could hardly be blamed for concluding that his native institutions were more benevolent" if he had "sniffed the faintest perfume of all these flowers of the Renaissance."[2]

A certain appreciation of violent men who "got things done" is not unique to Japan, yet violence always comes with ideological baggage. The military force employed by the three Japanese hegemons is seen as rational, necessary and secular, whereas the Iberians threatened to introduce a fanatical, hence illegitimate, conflict to the archipelago, one which would have impeded unification. Hall argued that "The spread of Christianity was basically divisive in its impact, giving rise to deep suspicions and tensions among Japanese of all classes." The implication is that the Warring States conflicts were less divisive because they were between Japanese, yet the internal social contradictions of medieval economic growth had been a major cause of those conflicts. Cullen claims that "Foreigners presented a military challenge because of the size of their vessels, their gun power and *their*

---

1 James Huffman, *Japan in World History* (Oxford: Oxford University Press, 2010), 57.

2 Sansom, *Japan: A Short Cultural History*, 423–24.

*sheer aggression towards Asians and one another.*"[3] By "foreigners" Cullen presumably means Europeans but it is unclear why the Japanese invasions of Korea in the 1590s (discussed below) do not qualify as "sheer aggression towards Asians." The image of Japan in China at this time was of a land of bloodthirsty pirates. The *Ming-shi* records that "The Japanese are by nature cunning...Given the opportunity, they take out their weapons and want only plunder." Valignano wrote that the Japanese "are the most warlike and bellicose race yet discovered on the earth." A Dutch observer noted that the Japanese are "lambs in their own country, but well-nigh devils outside of it." Adam Clulow suggests the violence employed by Japanese traders in Southeast Asia mirrored that used by Europeans but sets "the Japanese apart from rival Asian traders in this period."[4] The late sixteenth century saw a peak in piracy around the East China Sea. Chinese and Japanese edicts against pirates encouraged raiders to extend their activities even further afield and, in 1599, 1400 corsairs from Kagoshima attacked the Philippines, seizing two Chinese merchant ships in Manila harbour.

It would be obtuse to suggest that peace was not overall a good thing, yet what Morgan Pitelka calls the "hyper-violent pacification of Japan" came at a cost. Measures designed to root out Christianity involved strict surveillance over social life. Economic stasis required ever-increasing inputs of labour to stand still. Some Japanese scholars have proposed that the resulting "industriousness" was inherent in the national character, reflecting Japan's ability to realize itself without outside control. For Conrad Totman, it was a type of "self-exploitation," meaning greater control of the peasantry by the state. The "alternate attendance" system forced provincial

---

**3** L. M. Cullen, *A History of Japan, 1582–1941: Internal and External Worlds* (Cambridge: Cambridge University Press, 2003), 34, emphasis added.

**4** Adam Clulow, "Like Lambs in Japan and Devils outside their Land: Diplomacy, Violence, and Japanese Merchants in Southeast Asia," *Journal of World History* 24 (2013): 335–58.

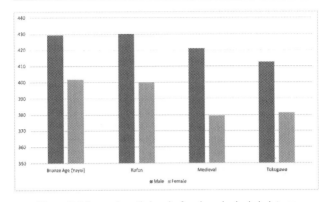

Figure 3.1 Femur length (mm) of archaeological skeletons (n=183) from Kyushu. Source: M. Hudson, "Stature and Standard of Living in Premodern Kyushu," *Journal of the Society of Human History* 11 (1999): 65–73.

lords and their retinues to spend one year in Edo after one year in their domains. While the French nobility was obliged to spend time at Versailles to receive favours from Louis XIV, the Tokugawa system kept the wives and children of lords as hostages in Edo. If the Warring States era had already put pressure on forests, rebuilding activities by the three hegemons led to unsustainable woodland use, necessitating strict conservation measures in the eighteenth century. As discussed in Chapter 4, the Christian Century saw the introduction of several new food crops, yet the average stature of Japanese people, a proxy for nutritional health, reached its lowest point since the Bronze Age (Figure 3.1). Popular resistance to the Tokugawa regime was expressed through thousands of uprisings and disputes.

The sixteenth century saw an increase in agricultural and other economic production in Japan as barons tried to finance their armies. This transformation included social mechanisms—some negotiated by peasants themselves—through which peasants were able to reduce the predatory impacts of large-scale warfare. The traditional (Confucian) separation between farmers and warriors was extended. Beginning in 1583, Hideyoshi's "sword hunts" prevented monks and peasants from carrying swords; protection would now be provided by the regime. Broadly speaking, therefore, political change over the Christian Century would seem to conform to an influential trend in historical scholarship which emphasizes the role of warfare in state formation. We will now examine this relationship in more detail.

## Firearms and the Military Revolution

The spread of firearms is one of the best-known aspects of Japan's Christian Century. According to the *Teppōki* (1606), the lord of Tanegashima bought one or two of the muskets carried by the Portuguese sailors who reached the island in 1543 for a large sum of money. A local blacksmith was instructed to make a copy, a task perhaps completed with the help of a Portuguese smith who arrived the following year. Tanegashima was connected to various religious and mercantile/pirate networks. By 1544, muskets were being manufactured in Sakai, Negoro, and Kunitomo near Lake Biwa. Sakai was described by Jesuit Gaspar Vilela in 1562 as "very extensive, exceedingly thronged with many rich merchants, and governed by its own laws and customs in the manner of Venice." Surrounded by moats for protection, Sakai had a population of around 30,000 and was known for forging swords and bells. Negoro temple was a centre for mercenary training and arms production in Kii province.

The introduction of muskets to Tanegashima has become overlain with various romantic stories, including those in the *Peregrinaçam*, an imaginative travel narrative penned by Portuguese merchant Fernão Mendes Pinto (1509?–1583). The picture of Japanese craftsmen diligently copying Western technology also resonates with popular ideas about Japan's later industrialization. Tanegashima was probably not the only source of guns in sixteenth-century Japan. Nor were firearms completely unknown in Japan prior to 1543. The Mongol invaders of the thirteenth century had employed ceramic projectiles filled with gunpowder. Firearms were used in the Ryukyus in the fifteenth century. An Okinawan surprised bystanders in Kyoto when he discharged a firearm there in 1466. On Okinawa Island, archaeological evidence supports the use of metal tubes (*hiya*) that shot stone, ceramic, and sometimes iron bullets. Despite these earlier weapons, the arquebus, soon followed by the musket, were new devices in the sixteenth century.[5]

The spread of Tanegashima muskets was due to a confluence of various technological and political circumstances. The island had iron sands used to produce high-quality iron that was already being sent to Sakai and Negoro for sword production. For firearms to work, gunpowder was also required. Sulphur was obtained from Satsuma-Iōshima Island located between Tanegashima and Kyushu, as well as from Iōtorishima in the Amami chain. Used to make gunpowder in China, sulphur had been exported from the Ryukyus since at least the eleventh century. Charcoal could be produced on Tanegashima and on the heavily forested neighbouring island of Yakushima. The latter had been invaded from Kyushu in 1542 but was quickly reconquered by the lord of Tanegashima in 1544. Saltpetre, the third ingredient of gunpowder, was initially imported from China and Siam. The Ōtomo domain bought saltpetre from the Portuguese. Lead for bullets was also imported, as was iron from Siam and India, until local production could support demand.

A great deal of debate over firearms in sixteenth-century Japan has revolved around the problem of historical agency. If

---

**5** For Okinawa, see Thomas Conlan, "Instruments of Change: Organizational Technology and the Consolidation of Regional Power in Japan, 1333–1600," in *War and State Building in Medieval Japan*, ed. John A. Ferejohn and Frances McCall Rosenbluth (Stanford: Stanford University Press, 2010), 124–58. On firearms in Iberia, see Antonio J. Rodríguez Hernández, "The Spanish Imperial Wars of the 16th Century," in *War in the Iberian Peninsula, 700–1600*, ed. Francisco García Fitz and João Gouveia Monteiro (Abingdon: Routledge, 2018), 267–99.

firearms were already known in Japan and were imported via various routes by the sixteenth century, did Europeans really play a significant role in the spread of the technology? Were the new weapons associated with a broader "military revolution"? Did Europeans already have a military advantage over Asia? Many contributions to the literature have played down the role of Europe. For instance, it is argued that tactical and political changes were transforming warfare in Japan *before* the introduction of firearms. Space precludes an exhaustive discussion here, but a few points can be mentioned. First, whether Europe had a military "advantage" in our period is a problem that needs to be kept separate from the diffusion of military technology. The adoption of firearms rapidly gave Japanese armies an upper hand in at least land warfare. While some weapons might have been obtained from overseas, there is no question that local production of firearms developed very quickly. By 1617, muskets were even being exported from Japan, the earliest example being a clandestine order by the English East India Company for twenty guns sent to Siam. Second, firearms played a role in the outcome of both specific battles and the larger balance of power in Warring States Japan. In 1591, Hideyoshi sent sixty thousand men to conquer the northern Tohoku region. His army attacked Kunohe castle with flaming arrows and guns, forcing its surrender in two days. Third, warlords in sixteenth-century Japan were in no doubt over the value of firearms, constantly instructing their subjects to bring guns to the battlefield.[6] Finally, ethnohistoric studies of Polynesia in the nineteenth century showing that muskets could have ideological power through their association with exotic outsiders suggests the need to consider firearms in Japan against a broader context of cultural transformation.

---

**6** Matthew Stavros, "Military Revolution in Early Modern Japan," *Japanese Studies* 33 (2013): 243-61; Yasushi Kawai and Karl Friday, "Medieval Warriors and Warfare," in *Routledge Handbook of Premodern Japanese History*, ed. Karl Friday (Abingdon: Routledge, 2017), 310-29.

Cannons were introduced to Japan as early as 1551 and were used in Nobunaga's first attack on Osaka in 1570. By the late sixteenth century cannons were widely used in siege warfare, generating a shift in castle architecture from earthen embankments to stone walls. The most iconic Japanese castles were constructed at this time as a response to the new weapons. Japan did not adopt the *trace italienne* style of flat fortifications with triangular bastions until much later. Goryōkaku in Hakodate and Tatsuoka in Nagano are examples of such pentagonal star-shaped forts built in the 1860s. The Iwata artillery battery in Kanzaki (Saga prefecture) was used for cannon practice from at least 1697. Iwata currently has a pentagonal shape and could be an early example of a Japanese star fort. I conducted archaeological prospection at Iwata in 2013. While this demonstrated the existence of several underground features, excavation is required to confirm the original shape of the site.[7]

Firearms also influenced naval warfare; as early as 1578, Nobunaga constructed armoured ships equipped with cannon. Europeans had some influence on Japanese ship-building more broadly at this time. Two European-style vessels were built in Japan under the direction of William Adams. One was loaned to the former governor of the Philippines and crossed the Pacific with a Japanese crew. The lord of Sendai, Date Masamune, had a 500-ton ship constructed under Spanish instruction. This also crossed to Mexico and then back to the Philippines where it was bought by the Spanish in 1616. In warfare, however, the Japanese navy was inferior and was badly defeated during Hideyoshi's invasion of Korea.

Our Century saw European influences on Japanese armour. Helmets of the originally Iberian cabasset style became widely used. Pointed cabasset helmets were thought better suited to deflecting bullets. A European inspiration has even been suggested for the exotic *kawari-kabuto* helmets

---

**7** M. Hudson and S. Handa. "Electrical Resistivity Surveys at the Iwata Artillery Site: A Preliminary Report," [in Japanese] *Bulletin of the Center for Regional Culture and History, Saga University* 8 (2014): 1–5.

with striking sculptures placed on top, which became popular at this time, though they were perhaps also a way to make commanders more visible through gun smoke. Sheet iron cuirasses, some at first imported from Europe, started to be used for protection against firearms instead of the earlier small iron or leather plates sewn together. Valignano gave Hideyoshi two Italian suits of armour in 1591. A piece of Italian armour given by Tokugawa Ieyasu to his son Yorinobu has ten dents from musket shots designed to demonstrate the bulletproof nature of the armour. Christian samurai would often decorate their armour with crosses, angels, or Latin writing such as the name Jesus.

## Religion, Violence, and "Pacification" in Late Medieval Japan

It is often claimed that, compared to Europe, religious violence was uncommon in East Asia. This is to misunderstand the nature of violence, which always draws on the social and cultural contexts where it is performed. The particular configuration of violence and religion found in, say, medieval Europe cannot be understood as a standard pattern that other societies approached or deviated from. The sixteenth century was a time of especially violent conflict in Japan and religion was one key axis through which that violence was conducted. While Christians bore a certain brunt, it was the new Buddhist movements described in the previous chapter that were the most affected, both in terms of sectarian disputes and conflicts with secular authorities. The unrest of the Warring States had initially worked in favour of the Christian missionaries since it gave them a range of potential allies. As unification progressed, however, the fate of Christianity increasingly came to depend on the whims of one warlord.

Christian-inspired violence in Japan included the destruction of Shintō shrines and Buddhist temples. Although the Iberian priests were not above encouraging such behaviour, Coelho's apologetic response to a question from Hideyoshi has a certain ring of truth: "Since the padres are on Japanese soil, where they have no political power whatever, they cannot use forceful methods against the wish of the local inhabitants...The destruction of Buddhist and Shinto temples is therefore the work of their converts, who are inspired thereto by spontaneous religious zeal." No doubt such zeal occurred on both sides. Valignano lamented the "custom of the Japanese to destroy everything they take, whether temples of their own sects or others, without paying the smallest respect to the very idols they worship."

The unification of Japan at the beginning of the seventeenth century occurred against the background of a range of European influences. Tokugawa rule was still opposed by Toyotomi Hideyori in Osaka castle, but the Great Exile of Christians out of Japan in 1614 shifted the balance of power as several senior Toyotomi followers left the country. Meanwhile Englishman John Saris had brought large quantities of military material to Japan, including six cannon, twelve tons of lead for bullets and cannonballs, and nearly 10,000 cubic litres of gunpowder. This was dangerous to store. The English first approached Hideyori, who declined to purchase on the grounds that it would be a provocation. When Ieyasu then agreed to buy the material, it was clear that he was planning an attack. Hideyori belatedly inquired about buying gunpowder and sent a message to Nagasaki urging Christian lord Takayama Ukon to return to defend Osaka. Both measures were too late, with Ukon having already sailed for Manila.

In 1614 and 1615, the Tokugawa regime laid siege to Osaka castle. The first campaign ended in a truce before eventual victory in June 1615. Hideyori is thought to have committed suicide; his body was probably burnt with the castle. Despite his father's anti-Christian measures, Hideyori had remained courteous to the missionaries and had a number of Christian samurai amongst his supporters. Morejón wrote that during the siege, "there were so many crosses, with the names of Jesus and Mary painted on their banners and pennants, and engraved onto their helmets and arms, that it is inconceivable that the shogun did not know about it." The cross had become an anti-Tokugawa symbol, yet Jerónimo Rodrigues, a

Jesuit with an extensive network of support across western Japan, claimed that "Even in the shogun's own army, many soldiers and captains openly declare themselves to be Christian, with the Holy Cross on their flags and rosaries around their necks for the whole world to see."[8]

The torture and execution of Christians in Japan during the second half of our Century has been widely discussed. While there are 2,044 "official" martyrs from Japan, some estimates of those killed reach as many as fifty thousand, excluding casualties from the Shimabara uprising discussed below. Comparisons with Europe involve tricky questions of definition, but the Japanese figures are large. In Spain, a territory almost twice the size of Japan during our period, the Inquisition executed around 1,000 people after 1520. There are estimates of around 5,000 martyrs in Europe as a whole from the 1520s into the seventeenth century.[9] All the churches that had been built in Japan were destroyed. Christian women were sometimes raped or sexually humiliated prior to execution; others were enslaved in brothels for failure to apostatise. After the first crucifixions in February 1597, the bodies of what became known as the Twenty-Six Martyrs were left exposed for months, with the last remains not being buried until October. Intended to show Hideyoshi's

---

**8** Ucerler, *Samurai and the Cross*, 271. On Rodrigues, see Reinier Hesselink, "A Letter from Jail: Christian Culture in Seventeenth-Century Nagasaki," *Journal of World Christianity* 7 (2017): 166–86.

**9** Hitomi Rappo, "History and Historiography of Martyrdom in Japan," in *Palgrave Handbook of the Catholic Church in East Asia*, ed. Cindy Y. Chu and Beatrice Leung (Singapore: Palgrave Macmillan, 2021), 1–38, here 11. The 50,000 estimate by Hubert Cieslik is cited from John Breen and Mark Williams, "Introduction," in *Japan and Christianity: Impacts and Responses*, ed. J. Breen and M. Williams (Basingstoke: Macmillan, 1996), 1–7. Figures for Europe are from Brad Gregory, "Persecutions and martyrdom," in *The Cambridge History of Christianity*, vol. 6, *Reform and Expansion, 1500-1660*, ed. Ronnie P-C. Hsia (Cambridge: Cambridge University Press, 2007), 261–82.

power, the display deepened the piety of the Nagasaki Christians. The collection of relics began soon after the deaths of the condemned: first blood soaked onto pieces of cotton and taffeta, then clothing and shavings from the crosses, and finally—as the bodies decomposed—actual bones. Such were the crowds attempting to collect relics that the Japanese guards had to build a surrounding fence. When the corpses froze hard in the cold, their preservation was deemed miraculous. By April, the bodies had thawed, and on Good Friday, blood started to drip from one of martyrs leading to huge crowds eager to witness the miracle.

Reinier Hesselink argues that the 1597 crucifixions radicalized the Christian community of Nagasaki.[10] The unmistakable similarities to the Passion led to a deeper engagement with the faith and the Imitation of Christ, but also to a heightened sense of community solidarity and of the turbulence of divine providence. Hesselink proposes that the extreme punishment administered to an adulterous couple in Nagasaki as described by Carletti was an example of such radicalization, an assault that perhaps drew on the European custom of the *charivari*.

Later executions were designed to prevent the collection of relics. One method was for the accused to be tied up in a sack and thrown into the sea. The remains of martyrs who were beheaded or burnt alive were similarly often disposed of at sea. In such cases, the returning boatmen had to strip and wash their bodies as well as the sacks and boats involved. Catherine, widow of a martyr named John Yukinoura, was tied naked to a tree and beaten, but the torturers attempted to prevent any blood from falling on the ground. A Tokugawa Inquisition (*shūmon aratame yaku*, "Office for Religious Reconversion") policed heresy, and a prison for interrogation and detention of Christians operated in Edo from 1646 until the late eighteenth century.

Despite—or because of—these measures, Christianity in Kyushu became re-imagined in ways that drew on popular

---

10 Hesselink, *The Dream of Christian Nagasaki*, 116.

practices in Catholic Europe, while adapted to the Japanese context. Describing 1614 processions in Nagasaki, Gabriel de Matos noted how some participants dressed in hemp bags tied up with ropes imitating the common method of execution. Other carried large crosses, or muskets "lashed to their legs so tightly that it looked like the barrels had penetrated their flesh." Others roped themselves together like slaves. Still others wrapped themselves in thorns or oyster shells, or used stones to mortify their flesh. One man even "carried two entangled snakes over his naked flesh that would bite him from time to time."

The causes of the Christian persecutions in Japan have been debated. Sansom argued that once Englishman William Adams had explained the attitude of Protestant states towards the church of Rome, Ieyasu "naturally" thought it desirable to exclude Iberian priests. Fróis believed that Hideyoshi's sudden attacks on Christians stemmed from his experience with the militant Buddhist sects, reporting an alleged statement by Hideyoshi on the day he issued a decree to expel the Jesuits:

> In part they appear to be similar to the sect of *Ikkō-shū*; but I consider them to be even more dangerous and prejudicial to the well-being of our realm. As you know, the sect of the *Ikkō-shū* was propagated only among workers and the lower classes.

> But these others [Jesuits], who are rooted in a higher knowledge, have taken a different path, working incessantly to secure the loyalty of the nobles...and the union between the two is stronger and much more solid than that of the *Ikkō-shū*. There can be no doubt that this is a very wise means with which to acquire kingdoms and conquer lands, for all those who belong to their sect blindly obey them.[11]

---

11 Ucerler, *Samurai and the Cross*, 197. A similar interpretation is advanced by Carol Tsang, "'Advance and Be Born in Paradise...': Religious Opposition to Political Consolidation in Sixteenth-Century Japan," in *War and State Building in Medieval Japan*, ed. J. A. Ferejohn

Timon Screech has discussed the role of Protestant England and the Netherlands in generating Japanese distrust over Iberian activities. In 1611, Ieyasu received two Dutch envoys at his castle in Shizuoka, a meeting arranged by Adams. The envoys delivered a letter from Maurice of Nassau explaining that the "Portuguese and Castilians will continue in their old habit of resorting to all possible manner of trickery and cunning" and warning in particular about the "double-dealing tricks of the Jesuits...who under the pretence of religious holiness seek to bring about a change of religion in Your Imperial Majesty's splendid Empire." This, the letter concluded, will "gradually tear asunder [your kingdom] and lead to partisanship and civil war." The dangers to Japan seemed to be confirmed by stories about the Spanish Armada. Adams had captained a supply ship during the Armada and later named his daughter Deliverance. In another audience with Ieyasu, Adams explained how a Protestant Wind had delivered England from the invasion. This seemed remarkably similar to the *kamikaze* ("holy wind") that had protected Japan during the Mongol invasion of 1281. All of this provided Tokugawa authorities with a blueprint to continue trade while excluding other, potentially disruptive social movements. According to Morejón, Ieyasu announced that "if the Kings and Princes of Europe do banish the Fathers out of their countries, I shall do them no injury to send them out of mine."

## Threats: Real and Imagined

The *threat* of invasion—real or imagined—has been a powerful motif in Japanese history, applied to T'ang China in the eighth, the Mongols in the thirteenth, and America and other Western powers in the nineteenth century. The idea that Europeans posed a serious threat to Japan in the late sixteenth century is also common in the literature. But how

and F. McCall Rosenbluth (Stanford: Stanford University Press, 2010), 91–109.

real was that hazard? There is a temptation here to confuse the sixteenth and nineteenth centuries, two very different periods in terms of ideology, economy, and technology, not least with respect to the time required for communications.[12] Continual wars in the archipelago limited any military options available to Europeans. Japan's highly militarized culture and rapid adoption of firearms made formidable battlefield opponents. How Europeans should react to local conflicts was a matter of debate and the Jesuits were aware of the dangers in taking sides, for example in wars between Christian and non-Christian lords. Valignano reminded his Fathers that "One should be very careful not to give advice either to wage war or to make peace. When it is inevitable to come to the aid of Christian Lords, it should be done so as not to alienate other Lords or declare ourselves as auxiliaries in war."

Nagasaki was the only major European settlement in Asia without a permanent military garrison. Ōmura Sumitada, the local baron baptized as Bartolomeu in 1563, attempted to defend Nagasaki as a Christian city with the help of the Society of Jesus, which assisted in the provision of firearms. The vulnerability of Nagasaki was demonstrated in 1573 when it was attacked by Fukabori Sumimasa, described by Fróis as a "great pirate" and "avowed enemy of God's laws." The following winter the city was besieged by another baron in league with Fukabori, forcing the construction of fortifications. On this occasion Nagasaki was saved by the tenacious defence by its Christian population. By 1580, however, the military position of Sumitada had become so weakened that, in a remarkable arrangement, he submitted to the Ryūzōji clan while handing over Nagasaki to Jesuit control. New perimeter fortifications were quickly added and Gaspar Coelho (ca.

---

12 In the late sixteenth century, letters from Portugal took two years and four months to Japan via Africa and India; the return journey was slightly quicker, at between eighteen and twenty months. The shorter (fourteen months) Spanish route via Manila and Mexico was also used on occasion: Ucerler, *Samurai and the Cross*, 99–100.

1529–1590), head of the Jesuit mission in Japan, wrote four times to the governor of the Philippines asking for help building a fortress in Nagasaki and two or three hundred Spanish soldiers to man it. This would have established a small military base in Japan, but nothing more: continual conflicts between the Kyushu barons ruled out further expansion.[13] Coelho's requests were rejected. Valignano concluded that in merely discussing these proposals, Coelho encouraged Hideyoshi's "persecution against the Society and the Christian community" because he moved him "to imagine that the Fathers possessed more power than they actually did." In 1587, Hideyoshi captured Kyushu and promptly took over Nagasaki from the Jesuits, destroying its fortifications.

Any discussion of the military threat posed to Japan by Europe during the Century needs to mention Alonso Sánchez's utopian scheme for a joint Iberian-Japanese invasion of China. A Spanish Jesuit, Sánchez (1547–1593) had worked in Mexico before leaving for the Philippines in 1581. That same year saw the union of the Spanish and Portuguese crowns, a development ironically precipitated by the death of King Sebastian of Portugal in an ill-planned attempt to conquer Morocco. Sánchez's plan, promoted in audiences with popes and kings, was for an expeditionary force of ten to twelve thousand men sent from Spain (with as many Basques as possible), to be combined with five or six thousand Visayans from the Philippines and a similar number of Japanese mercenaries. The military wing of this expedition, it was suggested, was not designed to conquer outright but to provide protection for propagation of the faith.

The background to this *empresa de China* has been analysed in detail by Antoni Ucerler. Two aspects are relevant here. The first is that the dreams of conquest derived from the *weak* position of the Iberians in Asia. The precarious situ-

---

**13** The role of Christianity in the micro-politics of late sixteenth-century Kyushu is described by Stephen Turnbull, *The Lost Samurai: Japanese Mercenaries in South East Asia, 1593–1688* (Barnsley: Frontline, 2021), 32–46.

ation of the Spanish in Manila, where only 600 soldiers were stationed, had already led to a 1580 proposal to abandon the Philippines altogether. Whatever success the Church had enjoyed in Asia could, it was understood, be rapidly over-turned by native resistance. The unusual position of Japan in this respect forms the second point. Of all the early Iberian colonial enterprises, Japan was the only place where military support was absent. Instead, explained Sánchez, Catholic suc-cess in Japan was due to "other arms that are equally strong if not stronger against the pagans, namely those of greed." If the Japanese no longer became interested in trade, the mis-sion would falter. While the idea of an invasion of China may have been completely fanciful, the problem of protection for Europe's distant colonies was a real issue. Sánchez seems to have been an eloquent speaker and obtained some support for his project. But he also met strong opposition. Valignano warned against military conquest of Japan: there is no "gain to be had there worthy of pursuit, for the land is the most barren and poor that I have ever seen. Moreover, it is a land that cannot be conquered for the great power they wield and the continual exercises in arms they engage in."[14] Sánchez's last audience with Philip II took place in August 1588 as news arrived of the defeat of the Spanish Armada. Long distrustful of plans to invade China, Philip was now in no position to con-sider the matter any further.

Small-scale Iberian military expeditions in eastern Asia did not come to a complete end. In the 1590s, a Spanish attack in Cambodia employing Japanese mercenaries led to disaster. The Spanish garrison at Manila also needed the help of Japanese mercenaries in its bloody suppression of a rebellion by the Sangley Chinese in 1603. Nevertheless, it remained more likely that Japan would invade the Philippines than vice-versa. Archbishop Benavides reported in 1595 that the Tagalogs had asked the Japanese to liberate them from

---

**14** Ucerler, *Samurai and the Cross*, 119. Valignano's clearly exaggerated first point reminds us of the need for caution regarding early European accounts of economic productivity in Japan.

their Spanish oppressors. Before his campaign in Korea, Hideyoshi had considered an attack on Manila, but Japan's naval defeats on the peninsula demonstrated the problems likely to be encountered on such a distant maritime invasion. An expedition to conquer Taiwan in 1616 seems to have been authorized by Ieyasu as a way to restrict the power of the wealthy Nagasaki Christian Murayama Tōan Antonio. While the expedition ended in disaster, it is unclear to what extent the Tokugawa regime might have invested in maintaining a colony on Taiwan. As late as 1637, however, the third *shōgun* Tokugawa Iemitsu was still considering a Japanese invasion of Luzon, ostensibly to prevent Spanish missionaries from reaching Japan. Though the Dutch announced their support for this invasion, the plans were brought to an end by the Shimabara uprising.

A peasant revolt in the Shimabara area of northwest Kyushu began in 1637. Over-taxation and poverty were the main causes but the rebellion quickly took on a Christian aspect. Failing to capture Shimabara castle, the rebels barricaded themselves in an abandoned nearby castle at Hara. Archaeological excavations have revealed a number of Christian objects from Hara castle, including a medal with Christ on one side and the Virgin Mary on the other, and crucifixes and discs made from bullets, together with a sandstone mould for casting the discs. The Tokugawa regime sent 120,000 troops but they were forced to wait until the rebels ran out of food in April 1638. Dutch help was sought in bombarding Hara castle from the sea. An estimated 37,000 rebels, including women and children, were then slaughtered after the castle was captured. Four decades after the Japanese invasion of Korea, Shimabara showed the weakness of Tokugawa forces.

If care is needed not to exaggerate the military threat posed by Europe, there is no question that Christianity provided a useful ideological peril for the Tokugawa regime. Two main periods of anti-Christian propaganda can be recognized in Japan. The first was in the mid-seventeenth century, when the Tokugawa government was being consolidated, but *after* Christianity had officially been eradicated from the country.

This was followed in the nineteenth century by a second phase during the decline of the Tokugawa and the establishment of the Meiji nation-state. In *Ideology and Christianity in Japan* (2009), Kiri Paramore argues that in both cases the most strident anti-Christian discourse was produced when there was no direct threat from the religion. This political use of Christianity was noticed in the 1960s by Masao Maruyama who posited an early modern system of social control based on the suppression of religion in favour of secular authority, a theme taken up by numerous historians, including Akira Hayami who stressed that the Christian Century was when Japan became "worldly not religious."[15] After its disastrous invasion of Korea, Japan even used Christianity as an imagined threat to repair relations with Korea and China. Letters to Korea in 1639 extolled Tokugawa "sternness" in combatting the "vile" and "base doctrine" of Christianity. The Koreans were unimpressed by such claims; when forced to discuss Christianity, a Korean embassy to Japan in 1643 replied that it had never heard of the religion until mentioned by the Japanese.[16]

## Women as "Threat" in the Christian Century

The question of threats during our Century also requires consideration of the position of women in the transition between medieval and early modern Japan. Haruko Ward argues that the remarkable success of Christianity in sixteenth-century Japan owed a great deal to the "unprecedented apostolate" of female believers. The Tokugawa regime saw this as such a threat that it suppressed women's activism under a Neo-Confucian ethos for over two centuries.[17] Contemporary Jesuit sources provide contrasting perspectives on Japanese

---

15 Akira Hayami, "Japan: Sixteenth, Seventeenth and Eighteenth Centuries," in *History of Humanity*, ed. Peter Burke and Halil Inalcik, vol. 5 (Paris: UNESCO, 1999), 344–57.

16 Toby, *State and Diplomacy*, 105.

17 Ward, *Women Religious Leaders*, 289.

women: admiration of the intellectual and spiritual engagement of some, but fear of the liberty, magic or "witchcraft"
of others. The freedoms enjoyed by Japanese women astonished Europeans such as Fróis, who claimed they were "free
to go where they please without their husbands' knowledge";
and that unmarried girls did the same without informing their
parents. After marriage, women retained their own property
and "sometimes the woman lends hers to her husband at
exorbitant rates of interest." Given the strict limits on female
behaviour introduced by the Tokugawa regime, Japanese
historians were long sceptical of Fróis's comments, but have
recently accepted their essential veracity. Fróis was also an
unexpectedly keen observer of Japanese women's fashion,
noting how they purchased "many wigs brought through trade
with China" and were so fond of make-up that while "In Europe
one case of face powder would be sufficient for an entire
kingdom; in Japan, despite importing many boatloads from
China, there is still a shortage." The Chinese "wigs" may have
been hairpieces made from yak hair. While clearly exaggerated, the comments on face powder index European *querelle
des femmes* debates over female vanity, yet display Fróis's
detailed knowledge of the commercial background involved.

Notwithstanding what, from an Iberian perspective,
seemed like considerable social freedoms for Japanese
women, their traditional religious status was more con-
strained. Japanese religions saw women as impure due to
menstruation and childbirth. The Buddhist "blood bowl sutra"
(*ketsubonkyō*), which reached Japan in the fourteenth century, taught that women must suffer in a "blood lake" after
death and offered them little hope of salvation. This was
probably one reason why Japanese women were attracted to
an apparently more inclusive Christianity. Japanese women
engaged with Christianity in a variety of ways. Some followed
men in their embrace of popular expressions of piety, including self-flagellation and hair shirts. Although there were no
Christian nunneries in Japan at this time, a convent-like organization known as the *Miyako-no-bikuni* (Nuns of Miyako) was
founded in Kyoto in 1600 by Naitō Julia (ca. 1566–1627). These

nuns were tortured and expelled to the Philippines in 1614. Other Christian women took vows of perpetual chastity and lived in seclusion at home (also a Buddhist practice) or sometimes in like-minded groups of pious women (*recogidas*).[18]

One of the most remarkable Christian women in sixteenth-century Japan was Hosokawa Tama Gracia (1563–1600). In 1582, Tama's father had been the key figure behind the assassination of Oda Nobunaga. Her husband immediately divorced her as a result, but kept her hidden in a mountain village. Pardoned by Hideyoshi two years later, Tama was restored to her husband in Osaka, where he kept her secluded and became increasingly abusive. Hearing news of Christianity, Tama secretly attended a mass in 1587 where she interrupted the sermon by *irmão* Takai Cosme with numerous questions. A few months later, Tama was baptized as Gracia. Fróis described Tama Gracia as having the mind of a *monstro* or "monster." Ward explains this term as meaning an extraordinary woman who surpassed her nature—which was to be intellectually inferior to men. For Fróis, her intellect could be linked with the European humanistic tradition of scholarly analysis of source materials. Christian theology seems to have provided Tama Gracia and her female associates with a liberating autonomy, even as the Jesuit fathers encouraged her to stay in her abusive marriage. Tama Gracia's "self-sacrifice" provided an effective model for both Jesuit and Confucian discourse, but the details of her life and violent death continue to be debated by historians.

In the Jesuit imagination, the most dangerous woman in sixteenth-century Japan was the former wife of Christian lord Ōtomo Sōrin (1530-1587). Her maiden family name was Nata but the personal name of this lady, who died in 1587, is not recorded. In Jesuit sources she is known as "Jezebel."

---

**18** As far as is known, no European nuns (or other women) reached Japan during the Christian Century. At least two European nuns are depicted on Japanese screen paintings walking together with Jesuit priests, but it has been argued that these were imagined by Japanese painters; see Ward, *Women Religious Leaders*, 75–77.

The Nata family were high priests of Hachiman, a powerful Shinto community associated with the god of war and seen as a protector of the nation and imperial family. Jezebel also supported esoteric Shingon Buddhism and its training of *yamabushi* mountain ascetics, who were regarded as "allurers and sorcerers" (*embaidores e feiticeiros*) by the Jesuits. Jezebel's religious background led her to regard Christianity as a political threat to Japan as well as a theological danger to her beliefs on female salvation via the Kumano school of Shingon. The Jesuits feared Jezebel as an embodiment of the most superstitious and idolatrous aspects of Japanese religions: sorcery, spirit possession, and loose morals. Their background and training afforded the Jesuits little doubt that they were dealing with witchcraft and the work of the devil.

### Colonialism in the Sixteenth–Seventeenth Centuries: Comparing Europe and Japan

During the period considered in this book, Japan attempted several colonial expansions. The most grandiose—and ultimately disastrous—was Hideyoshi's invasions of the Korean peninsula in 1592 and 1597. This was the largest war anywhere in the world in the sixteenth century, involving perhaps half a million combatants. The motives behind the invasion are much debated. Hideyoshi told Fróis about his plans to conquer Korea and China as early as 1586. A few years later, Hideyoshi wrote to the Viceroy of the Indies setting out an almost theological vision of world unity. "I am *tenka* [the realm, literally 'that under heaven']," he wrote. "Men are not men: I am mankind....Japan is not my country, China is not my country: China, India and Japan are all my body."[19] Hideyoshi also spoke of the "punishment" of the Chosŏn dynasty, a concept which led to the merciless slaughter of Korean people. His goal was conquest and various plans were made for colonial rule.

---

**19** Brett L. Walker, *A Concise History of Japan* (Cambridge: Cambridge University Press, 2015), 116.

Muskets proved key to the initial success of Japanese troops who reached P'yŏngyang in two months. Korean councillor Yu Sŏngnyong recorded that Japanese muskets "came like the wind and the hail." Although the Japanese were eventually defeated with the help of Ming China—and the death of Hideyoshi in 1598—the Korean peninsula was devastated. The enormous costs of the invasion were offset by the pillage of people and products. Perhaps 50,000 captives were brought back to Japan. Some were eventually returned to Korea, some remained in Japan, while others were sold as slaves. The Portuguese in Japan had at first traded primarily in Chinese slaves, but Japanese captives from the incessant wars between barons came to predominate from the 1570s, while large numbers of Koreans entered the market following Hideyoshi's invasions. Already in the 1580s, the price of a Japanese slave in Kyushu was considerably lower than that for a cow. The price for Korean slaves became so low that some were purchased by Africans who were themselves slaves of Portuguese owners.

The Korean war generated considerable interest from the Society of Jesus for its potential to spread the faith on the peninsula. Christian samurai participating in the invasion were accompanied by Spanish Jesuit Gregorio de Céspedes. While the conflict provided little opportunity for missionary work, it temporarily deflected persecutions in Japan and resulted in the mostly voluntary baptism of thousands of Korean captives after their removal to Kyushu. The trauma of war and enslavement perhaps encouraged the evangelization of these Koreans.

A much more successful Japanese colonial enterprise occurred in the Ryukyus. In 1609, the islands were invaded by the Satsuma domain of southern Kyushu. Ieyasu had authorized Satsuma's invasion, ostensibly to secure Japan's southern border against a possible Iberian attack. Although recent research has nuanced earlier views that Okinawans were reduced to virtual slavery as a result, profits from both foreign trade and agriculture were siphoned off by Satsuma. Sugar production in the Ryukyus became a lucrative business. Satsuma also took over responsibility for suppressing Christianity. Although commoners were not required to register with a Buddhist temple as in Japan, a religious census and the five-household system (which shifted responsibility for crimes away from individuals towards collective liability) were introduced.

The strategic location of the Ryukyus between Kyushu and Taiwan generated early interest in Europe. The first information about the islands—which Europeans called Lequios—reached Vasco da Gama in 1498 from his Omani pilot Šihāb ad-Din, also known as Ibn Mājid. Around 1545, Charles I even received a proposal to annex the islands. During our Century, however, Europeans made few attempts to trade or proselytise in the Ryukyus. The English were attracted by the possibility of obtaining amber, textiles, ambergris, and cowrie shells (widely used as money in Southeast Asia) but were unable to develop the necessary Ryukyuan connections before the English East India Company ceased activities in Japan.

Another important area of Japanese colonial expansion was Hokkaido, then known as Yezo.[20] Shinichirō Takakura assigns 1514 as the key date when the Kakizaki clan (re-named Matsumae after 1599) became *de facto* rulers of Japanese settlers in the southwest of the island, an area known as the *Wajinchi* ("land of Japanese people"). As in the Ryukyus, trade was the main Japanese interest. Most trade goods were provided by the native Ainu but gold was mined by Japanese settlers. The importance of the Hokkaido trade was noted by several Europeans. John Saris explained that "Necessaries for the bellie and the back are most vendible to [the Ainu]," mentioning rice, cotton, iron and lead. The Ainu traded salmon and other dried fish "which the Iaponners rather desire then silver." The *Wajinchi* grew larger over time. In 1672, it covered an area of 3,374 km². By the early eigh-

---

**20** Jesuit observers speculated as early as 1564 that the name Yezo might be related to Jesu. The native name for Hokkaido was first recorded in 1591 by Ignacio Moreira, who rendered it as *Ainomoxiri*.

teenth century it had a year-round population of 15,530 and by the end of that century there were more Japanese than Ainu in Hokkaido.

Prior to the Tokugawa "closed country" edicts, numerous Japanese had settled and traded across eastern Asia. The biggest diaspora community was in the Philippines, where there were around 3,000 Japanese in 1606. Other Japanese towns were found in Hoi An, Tonkin, Ayutthaya, Phnom Penh, Macau, and Batavia. Boxer suggested that without the closing of the country as a reaction to Christianity, early modern Japan would have been a very different place: Japanese settlements and overseas trade would likely have expanded and Japan might have followed Europe's path towards modernity much earlier than it did. Even if we accept critiques of the "closed country" paradigm by recent historians, this argument still deserves attention. Europeans in Asia in the sixteenth–seventeenth centuries were more interested in trade than territory. Trade was also important for the Japanese, but they also attempted to control territory, disastrously in the case of Korea, more successfully in Hokkaido.

## Christianity, State-Building, and the "Closed Country"

The Christian Century was a prelude to one of the most ideologically contested eras in Japanese history, the two centuries from the 1640s to 1850s when the nation isolated itself from the outside, a time that seems to stand in stark contrast to both the active modernization of the late nineteenth century and the earlier trading networks of the Middle Ages. However, relations with China and Korea continued, albeit in a strictly controlled form. It is the limitations placed on links with Europe (and thus also with the Americas) that have received most attention from historians. This section first discusses the immediate causes behind the isolation policies, before considering broader implications with respect to Tokugawa state-building.

In *The Shogun's Silver Telescope*, Timon Screech explores the influence of European confessional rivalry on seventeenth-century Japanese politics. Catholic success in Japan was well-known in England. In *Purchas his Pilgrimage*, published in 1613 before any English ship had returned from Japan, Samuel Purchas informed his readers how Jesuits were "busie intruding into affairs of state," employing "the carcass of reason" to "establish their new Romane Monarchie." Purchas understood how the Jesuit mission in this "furthest part of the world" was "so neere [central] to their industrie." At the end of August 1616, Richard Cocks, head of the English factory in Japan, arrived in Edo and began a series of important meetings, not least with *shōgun* Hidetada. On September 7, Cocks dined with the brother of the lord of Hirado. Later that night, he had a sudden visit by the secretary of one of Hidetada's chief councillors. In response to urgent questions, Cocks warned of the Jesuit threat, recently illustrated in England by the 1605 Gunpowder Plot. He explained to the secretary that "it were good he advized the Emperour [Hidetada] to take heed of [the Jesuits], lest they did not goe about to serve hym as they had donne the Kinges of England, in going about to kill & poizon them, or blow them up with gunpowder." The very next day, Hidetada issued a decree banning the "Sect of the Padres," a policy followed more strictly than previous prohibitions. Screech concludes that this timing was not coincidental.

In an irony not lost on contemporaries, the new regulations forced the English to close their regional offices, limiting them to Hirado. In 1619, *A Briefe Relation of the Persecution Lately Made Against the Catholicke Christians in the Kingdome of Japonia* was smuggled across the English Channel. Published in Saint-Omer (Pas-de-Calais), a centre for Jesuit publishing, the text stressed similarities between England and Japan, decrying how Protestant intrigue had undone decades of missionary work. A new edition of *Purchas his Pilgrimes* (1625) lamented the lost opportunities of the Japan trade, arguing that efforts in criticizing Rome should have been matched by support for the Church of England. While the situation in Japan already excluded such a direction, not for the first time in British history were the benefits of overseas trade undermined by disparagement of European rivals.

The closed country policies were proclaimed by the third *shōgun*, Tokugawa Iemitsu, a ruler whose sadistic character is stressed in contemporary European sources. Iemitsu's most radical measure was a 1633 decree preventing any Japanese, on pain of death, from travelling overseas or even from returning to Japan. In 1634, Iemitsu ordered the construction of an artificial island on mudflats in Nagasaki harbour. Measuring only 120 by 75 metres, Dejima became the single authorized base for European traders—now limited to the Dutch—from 1641.

We might consider the Tokugawa "closed country" as one of a series of religious expulsions in the early modern world. *Morisco* descendants of Muslims were forced out of Spain in 1609-1614. Later in the same century, Huguenots fled France for England and other Protestant countries. Persecutions against Japanese Christians forced many into exile in the north of the country or overseas. In the 1620s, there were 600 Japanese Christians in Siam. In 1621, over 1,800 Christian Japanese were living in Manila. Italian Jesuit Jerome de Angelis (1567-1623) was surprised to find a flourishing Christian community of 200 in Dewa province in northern Honshu in 1615. Two years later, a group of Japanese Christians fled to Hokkaido where they found work as gold miners. Until the late 1630s, there was more tolerance of Christianity in northern Japan; at least, edicts from Edo were enforced less vigorously. Crossing to Hokkaido in 1618, Angelis had refused to give alms to a Buddhist priest who, upon arrival, denounced him to the Matsumae authorities. However, the lord of Matsumae explained that although he was Japanese and the padres had been expelled from Japan, Angelis's entry was allowed since Matsumae was not subject to the *shōgun* or his laws. Historians have speculated that the Matsumae family themselves accepted aspects of Christianity, one piece of evidence being the letters T and H—considered as Christian symbols—carved onto two Matsumae gravestones. Gold miners in Hokkaido were initially excluded from persecution until 106 Christian miners were executed in 1639.[21]

Benjamin Kedar proposes that the corporate expulsion of an entire category of subjects beyond the boundaries of a polity is rare in world history, being largely a phenomenon of western Europe. The expulsion edicts of Tokugawa Japan constitute one clear exception, but Kedar argues that European precedents may have influenced the Japanese, a conclusion made at the time by Morejón.[22] In the Tokugawa case the expulsion even extended to non-Christian Japanese subjects who travelled abroad, a policy which mirrors the Catholic European concern with the spiritual purity of the realm discussed by Kedar. The closest Iberian parallel is the 1559 "quarantine" of Spain against Protestantism. A royal proclamation prohibited all Spaniards from leaving the country to "study, teach, learn, attend or reside in any university, school or college abroad"; individuals already outside Spain were required to return within four months. The Tokugawa measures were much more extensive and severe—and in a sense more "modern."

The role of religious reform in state formation was emphasized in German scholarship from the 1950s through the concept of *Konfessionsbildung* ("confession-building"), a term that avoided the partisan "Counter-Reformation" with its anti-modern implications. Confessionalization was proposed as a way for the state to further its control over the church and to discipline its subjects, generating a more modern form of political rule. This approach has some reso-

**21** Jaime González-Bolado, "Hasta los confines de Japón: un manuscrito inédito sobre el viaje de Jerónimo de Angelis a la isla de Hokkaidô (1618)," *Anuario de Historia de la Iglesia* 32 (2023): 399–421; Takao Abe, "The Seventeenth Century Jesuit Missionary Reports on Hokkaido," *Journal of Asian History* 39 (2005): 111–28. De Angelis's refusal to give alms to the Buddhist priest suggests arrogance sometimes got the better of stealth.

**22** Benjamin Kedar, "Expulsion as an Issue of World History," *Journal of World History* 7 (1996): 165–80.

nance in seventeenth-century Japan in Tokugawa attempts to unify the nation through a complex—though often expedient—mix of Buddhist, Confucian, and Shinto beliefs. Christianity had introduced ideas about transcendent loyalty that were regarded as incompatible with Tokugawa power. As mentioned, the Tokugawa also attempted to substitute religious with secular authority, though popular religious practices were maintained or even expanded in early modern Japan. The nature of Tokugawa authority has been much debated but it relied on all four of the sources of social power proposed by sociologist Michael Mann—ideological, economic, military and political—in order to administer what was increasingly seen as a geographically and ethnically coherent space.

## Conclusions

The early modern Japanese state was made through war, but helped by anti-Christian ideology. If the conflicts of the long Warring States era functioned like a violent game of musical chairs, reducing one-by-one the number of barons in military competition, the rapid spread of firearms in the late sixteenth century made the music run faster. Violence was also directed against autarkic merchant-pirates and Buddhist sects. The three hegemons attempted to make land and agriculture the primary source of political power—essentially a Confucian approach. Christianity, associated in sixteenth-century East Asia with mercantile trade, provided a convenient if largely manufactured threat that was manipulated as an ideological source of power for Tokugawa state-building. The continuation of Tokugawa anti-Christian discourse into the twentieth century still impacts historical debate over religious violence in Japan. The claim that "medieval Japanese society never experienced conversion enforced by violence" is posited as a main point of divergence with Europe, encouraging the assumption that "lack of a clear relationship between religion and violence is hence a crucial difference between European and Japanese societies of the medieval and early modern periods."[23] In contrast to such interpretations, we have seen how persecutions from the 1590s radicalized Japan's Christian communities. The Tokugawa state came to see the celebration of martyrdom as the most dangerous threat posed by the Christians. Conversion enforced by violence *did* occur in Japan with the forced re-conversion of hundreds of thousands of Christians in the seventeenth century. Nevertheless, the *Pax Tokugawana* is frequently imagined as deriving from the naturally peaceful nature of the Japanese people rather than from a politics of social control installed, at least in part, in reaction to European impacts.

---

**23** Fernanda Alfieri and Takashi Jinno, "Introduction," in *Christianity and Violence in the Middle Ages and Early Modern Period: Perspectives from Europe and Japan*, ed. Fernanda Alfieri and Takashi Jinno (Oldenbourg: De Gruyter, 2021), 1–15, here 7.

Chapter 4

# Global Goods in the Entangled World of Late Medieval Japan

The Christian Century marked one of three major stages of food globalization in Japan. The first was the Bronze Age when five cereals (barley, broomcorn millet, foxtail millet, rice, and wheat), domesticated pigs and chickens, and melon and peach were introduced. The third stage has been the modern period after the mid-nineteenth century. It was during the second stage, corresponding to our Century, that Japan saw the introduction of a suite of new, mostly American, crops, but also changes in the use of plants and animals that already existed in the country. Those changes were related to both cuisine and commerce: new tastes and ways of cooking became popular, just as international trading relations provided novel opportunities to sell foods such as wheat. Of course, Japan had not been completely isolated between the end of the Bronze Age and the sixteenth century. Several new crops and animals arrived during Late Antiquity and the Middle Ages, notably cattle and horses, Champa rice, and tea. The African domesticates cowpea (*Vigna unguiculata*) and sorghum (*Sorghum bicolor*) are also thought to have arrived from China during the Heian era (794–1185). Nevertheless, trade in foods and other goods became much more global in the sixteenth century.

This chapter discusses the varied impacts of trade and exchange during the Christian Century, examining the introduction of the new "global goods"—crops and changing foodways, syphilis, and a range of cultural borrowings. The exchanges encouraged transcultural expressions wherein Japan was entangled within a network of societies stretching from Iberia to India, Southeast Asia, and the Iberian colonies of the Americas. The evidence discussed in this chapter is often hidden in specialist journals and many aspects remain poorly known.[1] Despite Sansom's quip that sweet potatoes were more important to Japan than Catholic scripture, there have been few attempts to synthesize the material discussed below.

## Food

The new crops that reached Japan during the Christian Century are shown in Table 4.1. Some were brought by Iberian missionaries and merchants to recreate the Mediterranean foodways with which they were familiar.[2] Others were not necessarily directly introduced by Europeans, although written accounts sometimes encourage such an assumption. For instance, Richard Cocks wrote in 1615 that he planted sweet potato in Japan for the first time, but a slightly earlier introduction to southern Kyushu seems more likely. The first record of bitter melon (*Momordica charantia*) in Japan is from the Japanese–Portuguese dictionary published by the Jesuits in 1603, but this South Asian domesticate may have been known in the archipelago before that. Linguistic evidence is important in reconstructing the botanical histories summarized below. The Japanese language borrowed numerous words from Portuguese, Spanish, and then Dutch. Loanwords for plants can provide evidence of introductions even in the absence of other information. The spread of new foods at

---

[1] A recent overview of agriculture and the Columbian Exchange makes no mention of the spread of crops to Japan; see James F. Hancock, *World Agriculture Before and After 1492: Legacy of the Columbian Exchange* (Cham: Springer, 2022).

[2] Pedro L.R. Correia, "Father Diogo de Mesquita (1551–1614) and the cultivation of Western plants in Japan," *Bulletin of Portuguese-Japanese Studies* 7 (2003): 73–91.

Table 4.1. Cultivated plants introduced to Japan in the sixteenth and seventeenth centuries.

| Plant | Scientific name | Date of introduction |
|---|---|---|
| Sweet potato | *Ipomoea batatas* | Ryukyus by 1605, Kyushu by 1615 |
| White potato | *Solanum tuberosum* | 1598 (or possibly by 1576) |
| Maize | *Zea mays* | 1579 |
| Curcubits | *Curcubita* spp. | Mid-sixteenth century |
| Chilli | *Capsicum frutescens* | Before 1593 |
| Bell pepper | *Capsicum annum* | Late sixteenth century |
| Tobacco | *Nicotiana tabacum* | Late sixteenth century |
| Sugarcane | *Saccharum officinarum* | Early seventeenth century |
| Peanut | *Arachis hypogaea* | Before 1706 |
| Kidney bean | *Phaseolus vulgaris* | 1654 |
| Quince | *Cydonia oblonga* | Before 1599 |
| Papaya | *Carica papaya* | To Okinawa before 1719 |
| Tomato | *Solanum lycopersicum* | Second half of seventeenth century |
| Fig | *Ficus carica* | Before 1599 |
| Olive | *Olea europaea* | Several years prior to 1599 |
| Pomelo | *Citrus maxima* | Late seventeenth century? |
| Longan | *Dimocarpus longan* | Before 1708 |
| Sunflower | *Helianthus annus* | Seventeenth century |
| Mung bean | *Vigna radiatis* | Before 1695 |

this time was almost entirely *into* Japan; the Islands had few plants or foods not found elsewhere in Eurasia. However, the European encounter with Japan encouraged the spread of tea, which reached Holland in 1610. Soy sauce was also carried to Europe, being mentioned by John Locke in 1679.

The sweet potato was the most important new crop. While it had already reached Polynesia in the eleventh century, its introduction to Japan seems to have been the result of Spanish galleons carrying the plant from Mexico to Manila, from where it spread to China and then Japan. Sweet potato was known in the Ryukyus by at least 1605. Given the poor agricultural soils of the Ryukyu Islands, planting of the tuber was encouraged by the authorities. Sweet potato is mentioned as a snack in the *Matsuya kaiki*, an early seventeenth-century tea ceremony record. By the eighteenth century, sweet potato was cultivated more widely in Japan, especially in areas unsuited to rice.

Sweet potato spread more rapidly than the white potato, which is thought to have been introduced by the Dutch from Jakarta, hence the Japanese name *Jaga-imo* ("Jakarta tuber"). Genetic evidence supports an early introduction of European varieties.[3] The potato spread into the cooler regions of eastern Japan and was already being cultivated in Hokkaido in 1706 (Table 4.2). According to the *Hidagofudoki*, the potato was the fifth most important crop in the mountainous Hida region of Honshu in 1874 (after rice, barnyard millet, barley and soybeans).

*Cucurbita* squashes are another American domesticate that had a major impact on Old World foodways. Early modern Japan had at least four names for these plants: *bobura* (from Portuguese *abobora*), *nankin* ("Nanking"), *kabocha* ("Cambodia"), and *tōnasu* ("Chinese aubergine"). The latter term was also applied to the tomato, first brought to Japan by the Dutch in the seventeenth century, though only widely consumed from the late 1800s. Curcubits are said to have

**3** Kazuyoshi Hosaka, "Similar Introduction and Incorporation of Potato Chloroplast DNA in Japan and Europe," *Japanese Journal of Genetics* 68 (1993): 55–61.

Table 4.2 Earliest recorded dates from Hokkaido of crops introduced to Japan during the Christian Century.

| Crop | First recorded date of cultivation |
| --- | --- |
| Kidney bean | 1694–1696 |
| White potato | 1706 |
| Tobacco | 1717 |
| Maize | 1796 |
| Pumpkin | 1799 |
| Chilli | 1800–1802 |

Data from Tadashi Yamamoto, *Kinsei Ezochi nōsakumotsu nenpyō* (Sapporo: Hokkaido University Press, 1996).

reached Japan in the Tenbun era (1532–1555), spreading to Kyoto by the early seventeenth century and to Edo only in the Meiwa era (1764–1772). As shown in Table 4.2, however, they were already found in southern Hokkaido in 1799. *Curcubita* seeds have been discovered from at least sixteen Tokugawa-period archaeological sites, though none have been directly radiocarbon dated.

While various theories exist as to route(s) and chronology, chilli peppers were introduced to Japan during our Century. The *Tamon-in Nikki*, a diary written by monks of a Nara temple, mentions chilli in an entry for February 1593. In northern Japan, chilli is called *namban*, whereas *tōgarashi* ("T'ang or Chinese mustard") is common in western Honshu. *Capsicum* seeds have been recovered from eight archaeological sites in Japan, though none have been directly dated. Recent DNA analysis supports a trans-Pacific route for the diffusion of chilli to Japan.[4]

---

**4** Sota Yamamoto et al., "Genetic Diversity and Phylogenetic Relationships of *Capsicum frutescens* in the Asia-Pacific Region: The Pacific Dispersal Route," *International Journal of Historical Archaeology* (2024), https://link.springer.com/article/10.1007/s10761-024-00750-w.

Tobacco reached Japan in the late sixteenth century. In 1615, Richard Cocks wrote that the lord of Hirado had attempted to prohibit its use and cultivation, which greatly upset the Japanese since "men, women, and children, are besotted in drinking that herb; and, not ten years since it was in use first." Despite further bans, tobacco spread widely through Japanese society. Similar bans in Europe had been unsuccessful. In 1635, a Dominican prior from Barcelona complained that priests would even smoke at the altar.[5] The spread of tobacco in Japan can be traced archaeologically by pipes (called *kiseru* in Japanese, probably from Khmer *khsier*). A painting of Hideyoshi and the emperor watching Noh theatre dated to the 1580s or early 1590s shows audience members smoking exaggeratedly long pipes. Early seventeenth-century pipes excavated from Ainu sites in Hokkaido show that the custom spread very quickly to the north. Tobacco has been identified from DNA in dental calculus at a late Tokugawa cemetery in Tokyo.[6]

The tobacco trade within Japan generated an interesting series of events in 1685 when a Japanese vessel was shipwrecked off Macau. The crew explained that they had been blown off course bringing tobacco from Ise to Nagasaki. The Portuguese saw the return of the twelve Japanese castaways as an opportunity to re-open trade with Japan. Three months after the shipwreck, the *São Paulo* left Macau with the castaways. Reaching Kyushu three weeks later, the vessel spent two months in Nagasaki harbour, with the Portuguese crew (which included thirteen Africans and Asians) never being allowed onshore. The Japanese castaways were stripped naked to make sure they were not hiding anything. After detailed interrogation, they were permitted to return home, but the Portuguese aim of re-opening trade with Japan was unsuccessful.

---

**5** Henry Kamen, *The Phoenix and the Flame: Catalonia and the Counter Reformation* (New Haven: Yale University Press, 1993), 346.

**6** Rikai Sawafuji et al., "Ancient DNA Analysis of Food Remains in Human Dental Calculus from the Edo Period, Japan," *PLoS ONE* 15 (2020): e0226654.

Japan appears only once in Mintz's *Sweetness and Power*—as an example of an "ancient society" that had been *resistant* to food globalization, yet sugar had been used in Japan as a medicine since at least the eighth century. During our Century, sugar became widely used in Japanese cooking and large quantities were imported by Chinese, Dutch, and Portuguese traders. Together with soy sauce and *saké*, sugar remains a key ingredient in Japanese cooking. Sugarcane was cultivated in the Ryukyus from the beginning of the seventeenth century and soon became the main export commodity of those islands. The eighteenth-century *shōgun* Yoshimune (r. 1716–45) attempted to increase domestic production of Japan's main imports—silk, ginseng, and sugar. By the 1780s, it was said that consumption of domestically produced sugar had outstripped that imported from China, an achievement which required considerable coercion of peasant cultivators, especially in the Amami Islands.

Other plants that reached Japan during our period include quince, a favourite of Jesuit Diogo de Mesquita (1551–1614), Rector of the Nagasaki college. Quince was known in Japanese as *marumero* from Portuguese *marmelo*. Although a wild fig *Ficus erecta* is native to Japan, *F. carica* was brought on Iberian ships in the sixteenth century. In a letter of 1599, Mesquita expressed his satisfaction that one of the olive trees that had been brought from Europe had already borne fruit. Two decades earlier, Valignano had recommended that, while it was important to be careful about providing beef or pork to Japanese who were not used to eating them, it was acceptable to offer "very pure foods by which they will not be taken aback," a category which included "bread, sugar pastry, preserves, olives, and things of such nature."[7]

Several other New World crops were carried to Eurasia by Europeans but only later transmitted to Japan. The kidney bean is said to have been introduced in 1654 by a Zen monk named Ingen, leading to the name *ingen-mame* ("Ingen bean"). Papaya is recorded in Okinawa from 1719 but the

---

**7** *Sumario de las cosas de Japón*, cited from Elison, *Deus Destroyed*, 59.

date and route of its introduction are unknown. Peanuts are known from southern coastal China in the early sixteenth century and reached Japan by at least 1706. The Japanese name for cashew nut (*kashū*) is thought to derive from Portuguese *caju*, suggesting an early trade. Finally, the mung bean was domesticated in India around four thousand years ago but spread rather slowly to East Asia, perhaps due to climatic constraints. Earlier reports of mung beans from sites of the Japanese Neolithic Jōmon period have recently been discounted by archaeologists. The first written record of the bean from Japan dates to 1695. The timing and context of its introduction to the archipelago remain unclear, but a link with the international trade of our Century is a reasonable hypothesis.

## Domestic Animals and Meat Consumption

European contact increased meat consumption in Japan. Valignano explained that:

> The Japanese used to have a great revulsion from eating any kind of meat except game from hunting, and there was also a universal abhorrence of our kind of food. They were scandalized, in fact, to learn that Ours ate the flesh of cows and pigs, so that for a long time it was necessary for us to abstain from those things and eat their food...But what with the trade with the Portuguese, and the very long war which they have had in Korea, for some years past now the Japanese have been eating and enjoying poultry, pork, beef, and others of our dishes, so much so that there is hardly a banquet nowadays which does not include at least some of our things.[8]

João Rodrigues recounted how hens, pigs, and cattle kept at port cities to feed the Portuguese led to wider consumption

---

[8] Cited from J. F. Moran, *The Japanese and the Jesuits: Alessandro Valignano in Sixteenth-Century Japan* (Abingdon: Routledge, 1993), 55–56.

of these animals by the Japanese: "Not only the merchants who come from various places to trade with [the Portuguese], but also many others now eat these things. Even nobles and others do so under the excuse of regarding it as medicine and something new."

Some caution is required with respect to Jesuit writings on Japanese food because they primarily described aristocratic diets. An example is Valignano's insistence that the Fathers serve Japanese guests with meals comprising rice, soup, and three side dishes. This pattern formed a basis of the *wash-oku* ("Japanese food") cuisine inscribed as UNESCO Intangible Cultural Heritage in 2013, but food historians argue that such a menu only became common in home-cooking in the 1960s. Class differences in meat consumption likely also existed; residents of upland villages would have hunted on a regular basis, not least to protect their crops.

Meat-eating was sometimes used as polemic against Europeans. In 1586 and again the next year, Hideyoshi objected to the consumption of cattle and horses, proposing Europeans eat wild animals instead of beasts useful for agriculture and transport. While noting that they did not eat horseflesh—banned by the pope in the eighth century—the Jesuit response was guarded, at first stating that this was a matter for believers to decide themselves, then agreeing to avoid eating veal "in the future if the regent wishes it." Mihoko Oka suggests that Hideyoshi, already planning his invasion of Korea, was worried about maintaining agricultural production and his complaints about Portuguese involvement in slave trading similarly reflected his need for labour rather than humanitarian concerns.[9]

---

**9** A study of animals in premodern Japan erroneously claims Europeans engaged in "voracious consumption" of horsemeat; see W. Puck Brecher, *Animal Care in Japanese Tradition: A Short History* (Ann Arbor: Association for Asian Studies, 2022), 18. Brecher also emphasizes the "dietary freedoms" of Christianity, but it was perhaps the combination of fewer taboos over meat-eating with strict fasting regulations that appealed to the Japanese.

The domesticated chicken was introduced to Japan by at least the third century BC. For nearly two millennia thereafter, however, chickens remained rare and seem to have been primarily used for rituals and cock-fighting, a not uncommon pattern in other parts of Eurasia. Around the time of the Christian Century there was an increase in chicken bones found in archaeological sites in Japan. Historical records suggest an increase in egg consumption from the seventeenth century; chicken meat also became more widely accepted. The *Namban ryōrisho* ("Southern Barbarians' Cookbook"), a seventeenth- or possibly late sixteenth-century manuscript, includes a *paella*-like dish with chicken on a bed of rice coloured yellow with gardenia (probably an alternative to saffron, which seems to have been first imported to Japan later in the Tokugawa period). In 1652, Confucian scholar Hayashi Razan explained how chickens and eggs had long been prized in China, an argument which obfuscated any dangerous links with Christianity. Early Tokugawa sumptuary laws prohibited commoners from serving wild geese, duck, crane or swan, the fowl preferred in élite banquets; chicken may have served as a replacement for those birds.

Eggs were a key ingredient in many new dishes introduced by the Iberians, including *kasutera* (named after *Bolo de Castela*, "cake from Castile"), *bōro* (*bolo*, "cake"), and *tempura*. The *Harajō kiji* (1557) and *Taikōki* (1626) describe *kasutera* and *bōro* made with eggs and the *Ryōri monogatari* (1643), said to be Japan's oldest cookery manual, contains five egg dishes. Egg whites were added to smoothen sugar syrups for boiled sweets. Poet Matsunaga Teitoku (1571–1653) mentioned a "tub of eggs hardened in sugar" as a well-known souvenir of Nagasaki. The sixteenth century also saw a proliferation of recipes using eggs in Europe as Lenten restrictions were relaxed and this dietary culture seems to have influenced Japan.

The goat is another domestic animal that became more common in at least western Japan. Goats had sometimes been sent as gifts from continental rulers to the Japanese court; such gifts are recorded from 599, the early ninth century, 903,

909, 919, and 935. It is unclear whether this led to the raising of goats at the court or elsewhere. By the sixteenth century, however, more evidence is available. Andres de Aguirre
related an early contact with Okinawa in a letter dated 1584
or '85. Driven off course, a Portuguese ship reached an island
where they were welcomed as merchants. A Portuguese and
an Armenian from the boat were sent with gifts to the king who
lived in a large and magnificent residence (presumably Shuri
castle). The merchants sold their goods and were paid in silver. Aguirre states that the Okinawans "had pigs, goats, bulls
and wild boars, and ate much fish and fruit."[10] This would suggest that goats had already been introduced to the Ryukyus,
perhaps through trading contacts with Southeast Asia where
goats are known from Bali as early as the first century AD. In
Kyoto in 1613, John Saris bought "henns and phesants of the
best for iii pence a peece, pigges verie fatt and large xii pence
a peece, a fatt hogge v shillings, a good beefe, such as our
welch runts, at xvi shillings. A Goate iii shillings, Rice a half
pennie a pounde." Two years later, Richard Cocks recorded
that Chinese merchant Li Tan provided a leg of pork and a leg
of goat for a celebration in Hirado.

Goats were brought to Kyushu on European and Chinese
ships. Carl Thunberg (1743–1828), described how "every year"
the Dutch carried "calves, oxen, hogs, goats, sheep and deer"
to Nagasaki from Batavia for their provisions. These animals
were raised on Dejima and it is unclear to what extent they
escaped beyond. In 1605 a fellow Jesuit complained that Diogo
de Mesquita spent too much time in the garden raising geese
and goats, and that he made cheese from goat's milk.[11] Hen-

---

10 Josef Kreiner, "Notes on the History of European-Ryukyuan
Contacts," in *Sources of Ryūkyūan History and Culture in European
Collections*, ed. J. Kreiner (Munich: iudicium, 1996), 15–41, here 21.
Kreiner explains the role of Armenian traders in the Indian Ocean
after their kingdom had been conquered by the Ottomans in 1514.
One name for the Ryukyus at this time was Islas de Armenio,

11 Diego Pacheco, "Diogo de Mesquita, S.J. and the Jesuit mission
press," *Monumenta Nipponica* 26 (1971): 431–43.

drik Hamel, a Dutch sailor shipwrecked in Korea, wrote in 1668 that Japanese at Pusan traded goatskins to the peninsula.

## Fishing and Whaling

European accounts of late medieval Japan provide us with many interesting details about agriculture and foodways, but marine resources receive less attention. Fróis's *Tratado* noted the unusual seafood enjoyed by the Japanese: raw and fried seaweed, rotten fish tripe, and of course "raw" fish (which at the time was likely pickled or fermented in some way). Specific types of fish are rarely mentioned, though Fróis observed that while mullet was prized in Iberia, "in Japan, it is considered repugnant and food for the poor." *Mullus* sp. remains a delicacy in the Mediterranean, but the Japanese fish was probably *Mugil cephalus* (Japanese *bora*). As regards the fishing industry, Fróis remarked that in contrast to Europe, fishing was "considered lowly and an activity for base individuals" in Japan.

One interesting account of the marine economy comes from Angelis, who travelled to Hokkaido on a ship loaded with rice and *saké*, goods traded for dried salmon and herring, sea otter skins, and Chinese silks and glass beads (obtained from the Amur). According to Angelis, as many as a hundred Ainu ships would come to the Japanese enclave of Matsumae from eastern Hokkaido. Other vessels brought goods from the western ports of that island and thus presumably also from Sakhalin.

The unification of Japan under the Tokugawa encouraged commercialization of fishing, not least to provide food for the huge city of Edo, which had a million inhabitants by the eighteenth century, making it the largest city in the world. The "closed country" policies limited the size of boats that could be constructed. Pelagic species such as tuna were caught when they migrated along coastal currents but, unlike Europe, where late medieval fishing had shifted to offshore species, the Japanese fishing industry continued a primarily inshore focus. Nevertheless, a vibrant trade in dried marine resources to Ch'ing China developed at this time.

As in other parts of the world, opportunistic use of beached whales has a long history in Japan. However, the late sixteenth century saw a sudden shift to targeted, commercial whaling using harpoons. This whaling first emerged around 1570 in Ise Bay, partly stimulated by the need for new sources of fertilizer to support agricultural production.[12] The use of whale oil is mentioned by Rodrigues. The chronology here raises the question of possible Iberian influence. The Basques were the most active whalers in sixteenth-century Europe and were continually searching for new whaling grounds. Although I am unaware of any direct evidence linking Iberian and Japanese whaling at this time, the period from around 1600 saw a major expansion of commercial whaling right across the northern hemisphere and it seems parsimonious to include Japan in that broader trend.[13]

## Wheat and Japanese Overseas Trade

The Christian Century generated new opportunities for exports from the archipelago. The Spanish colony of Manila, established in 1571, became a major destination for Japanese as well as Chinese goods, including wheat. Wheat had been cultivated in Japan since the Bronze Age. From the eighth century, the Japanese state issued decrees encouraging cultivation of wheat and other non-rice crops. The arrival of Europeans in East Asian waters expanded the market for the cereal. The Iberians favoured wheat, not only for bread but also as biscuits for long sea journeys. Wheat was not grown in the Philippines and had to be imported. Antonio Morga, in the Philippines from 1595 to 1603, wrote that Japanese and Portuguese merchants sailed every year from Nagasaki:

---

**12** Fynn Holm, *The Gods of the Sea: Whales and Coastal Communities in Northeast Japan, c. 1600–2019* (Cambridge: Cambridge University Press, 2023), 30–33.

**13** See John F. Richards, *The Unending Frontier: An Environmental History of the Early Modern World* (Berkeley: University of California Press, 2003), 574–616.

"Their main goods are wheat of a very good quality which is much needed in Manila." Morga also mentioned dried meat, textiles, weapons, wooden furniture, and salted tuna. Valignano reported in 1593 that, "Usually, two or three Japanese ships sailed to the Philippines every year, in order to export biscuits, wheat flour, beef, and other foodstuffs....The Castilians welcomed their arrival, since these commodities are in short supply in the Philippines." In 1621 Japanese ships carried a range of provisions to Manila, including 947 bags of wheat flour, 49,900 pieces of biscuit, soy beans, oil, and pig's trotters.

During Hideyoshi's invasion of Korea, Japanese general Katō Kiyomasa sent a letter to his domain in Kyushu with instructions to launch a trading mission to raise funds for his struggling campaign. Katō wrote:

> I have learned that wheat flour is welcomed as export goods, so I order that wheat flour of 200,000 jin [about 120 tons] be loaded on board. Townsmen who are intending to go abroad together should be familiar with flour; question them on the manufacturing process of it. Do not fail to prepare wheat flour of 200,000 jin by levying it from peasants of our domain.

Katō's letter is interesting not least because its author, a Nichiren Buddhist, is represented in Jesuit sources as a forceful opponent of Christianity. Katō's letter does not specify the intended destination of his wheat, but Manila was the most likely candidate. The need to have the wheat properly milled into flour was noted. Small rotary querns had been introduced to Japan from China in the medieval era and used in the production of noodles. Florentine merchant Francesco Carletti, who visited Nagasaki in 1597, wrote that even though the Japanese

> have wheat, they do not make bread, though they eat it cooked into little cakes among the ashes and embers, as well as in various other ways. But most of it, made into flour by small wheels that they themselves turn with one hand, is sent out of the country, mostly being taken to be sold in

the Philippine Islands...where Spaniards live who buy it to make it into bread.

Carletti claimed that the trade in wheat "and other sorts of provisions and merchandise" generated profits of between 60 and 100 per cent.

Export of foodstuffs from Japan did not cease with the closed country edicts. In the seventeenth century, the Dutch exported rice, wheat flour, soybeans, dried fish, and other foods from Nagasaki, mainly to Batavia. As the Tokugawa government tried to limit the export of precious metals, dried seafoods for the Chinese market became a valuable substitute. These included kelp (*konbu*), sea cucumber (*trepang*), and abalone. This trade has important implications for Eurasian economic history and the "Great Divergence" debate. While historians such as Eric Jones have suggested that premodern East Asia lacked a long-distance trade in basic foodstuffs, the movement of wheat, fish, and other foods from Japan and China disproves this claim.

## The Influence of *namban* Cuisine

Food is one of the most debated aspects of Japanese identity. While, as mentioned above, a "traditional" *washoku* diet has been recognized by UNESCO, this diet was not widespread in premodern Japan, at least beyond élite circles. Japanese writers emphasize the introduction of three unusual elements into Japanese cuisine during the Christian Century: meat, oils, and spices. The *lack* of these items is therefore seen as defining "traditional" Japanese foodways.

According to Jesuit accounts, Japanese élites were at first disgusted at European customs and behaviour. Ōtomo Sōrin told Valignano "how often he was so infuriated and disgusted when leaving one of our houses that he was determined never to come back." The Iberians quickly became aware how Japanese food and table manners differed from Europe; the Iberian habit of eating with the hands instead of chopsticks aroused particular shock. Cleanliness and manners were perceived as stumbling blocks to conversion and the Jesuits rapidly made efforts to learn Japanese manners. The Japanese culture of banquets and entertaining was observed in exhaustive detail by Rodrigues. Spanish merchant Bernardino de Avila Giron (in Japan 1597–98) wrote "I will not praise Japanese food for it is not good, albeit it is pleasing to the eye, but instead I will describe the clean and particular way in which it is served." According to Valignano, the Japanese considered the Europeans as "slobs" (*sucios*) and he insisted that Jesuits follow local customs of using chopsticks, eating rice instead of bread, and consuming less meat. Fróis noticed that table manners had a distinctive cultural side: "Among us, making loud noises while eating and completely draining a cup of wine are considered slovenly; the Japanese consider both of these things to be refined manners." Nevertheless, European foods attracted growing interest and a number of dishes of Iberian origin were adopted. Later adaptations to local taste are sometimes presented as evidence that European influence on foodways in late medieval Japan was weak, but such changes are common in culinary history. In the Nagasaki recipe *hikado* (from Portuguese *picado* "mince"), beef was replaced by sliced tuna, which was simmered instead of being sautéed in oil. A fried pancake called *filhos* in Portuguese became a pattie with crushed tofu and pieces of vegetables known as *hirōsu* (or *hiryōzu*) in western Japan and *ganmodoki* in the east of the country. The 1784 *Takushi-shiki* explains this recipe as including a dough made from eggs and glutinous rice flour. Fried in oil, the pattie was topped with syrup in the Portuguese style. *Tempura* is today one of the best-known Japanese foods. The usual etymology relates the word to the fasting times (*temporas* in Portuguese and Spanish) during Ember Days. In Japan, there seem to have been a range of fried dishes under the category of *tempura*; changes were made over time to suit the Japanese market.

Frying fish and vegetables in a batter made from flour, eggs, and water (or milk) was often associated with Jewish and Muslim cuisines in Iberia. Although oil from sesame, *Perilla frutescens*, colza, and other plants had been known in Japan and used for handicrafts, cosmetics, and lighting as well as for consumption, the increase in the use of oil for frying marked a major shift in Japanese food history. Dorian Fuller and Michael Rowlands have proposed that premodern Eurasia can be classified into several different culinary zones which date back to the Neolithic.[14] East Asia, where ceramics appeared very early, was characterized by foods that were boiled or steamed. West Asia, and later Europe, by contrast, were home to a tradition of grinding, roasting and baking in ovens. Fuller and Rowlands argue that these culinary zones remained stable for long periods *despite* the exchange of new crops. From that perspective, the Christian Century marks an important transformation in culinary practices in the Japanese archipelago. Nevertheless, the technology of oven-baking was not easily adopted in Japan. Early recipes for *kasutera* and *bōro* describe placing the mix on a fire and then setting another pot filled with hot coals on top. The 1718 *Kokon meibutsu gozen gashi hidenshō* ("Secret Writings on Famous Japanese Confectionary New and Old") explains how to build an oven to bake bread outside. The detailed explanation suggests such things were rare at the time.[15] Ovens were not widely found in Japanese homes until the end of the twentieth century.

The *Namban ryōrisho* describes many new dishes, especially for confectionary. Eggs were a common ingredient: the recipe for *kasutera* asks for ten. Some ingredients and instructions in this work mirror those of medieval Iberian cookbooks, for example the use of cinnamon, cloves, garlic, and black pepper as spices (these were already known in Japan); the dyeing of food; sugar sprinkled on top of savoury dishes; tear-

---

**14** Dorian Fuller and Michael Rowlands, "Ingestion and Food Technologies: Maintaining Differences over the Long-Term in West, South and East Asia," in *Interweaving Worlds: Systemic Interactions in Eurasia, 7th to the 1st Millennia BC*, ed. Toby Wilkinson, Susan Sherratt, and John Bennet (Oxford: Oxbow, 2011), 37–60.

**15** Eric Rath, *Food and Fantasy in Early Modern Japan* (Berkeley: University of California Press, 2010), 97–101.

ing chicken into small pieces; and stuffing chicken with boiled eggs. While some Japanese insinuated that Christian priests used sweets and wine to attract followers to their sect, many Iberian foods were rapidly accepted in Japan without religious overtones, though strict sumptuary laws controlled the austere diet of peasants. Regulations in 1642 and again in 1649 prohibited peasants from making or purchasing wheat noodles or tofu, and from brewing or buying alcohol. By the end of the Tokugawa period, the label *namban* had lost its dangerous connotations and was increasingly applied to "exotic" dishes, a commodity-branding that continues today. *Chikin namban*—fried chicken with a vinegar or tartare sauce—was invented in Kyushu in the late 1950s and is now a common item on Japanese menus.

## Mining Technology

The sixteenth century saw a boom in metal mining in many parts of the world. Silver was the key commercial enterprise linking Japan, China, the Philippines, and the New World. The seventeenth century then saw a massive increase in the production and export of copper from Japan. Gold and silver also financed the armies of competing Japanese warlords. By no means all technological developments associated with mining at this time came from Europe or European colonies, but one such example was mercury amalgamation, used at the Iwami silver mine by the early seventeenth century. Ieyasu had met with Rodrigo de Vivero, former governor of Manila, who was shipwrecked near Edo in 1609. Vivero's knowledge of mining was considered especially important and Ieyasu hoped for 200 Spanish miners to teach the mercury amalgamation process. Ōkubo Nagayasu, a former Noh actor and lord of Hachiōji, was appointed supervisor for gold and silver mining at Iwami, Izu, and Sado. Nagayasu's contacts with the Spanish may have enabled him to introduce the amalgamation method. While this method was ultimately found to be too expensive, given that mercury was rare in Japan, Nagayasu himself became extremely wealthy. After his death in 1613, his extravagant lifestyle was discovered to be based on fraudulent accounting. His seven sons were sentenced to crucifixion and Nagayasu's corpse was dug up and subjected to the same punishment. Although there is no clear evidence that Nagayasu was himself a Christian, he was accused, probably unjustly, of acts of treason in association with Christian powers.

The Sumitomo copper refinery established in Osaka in 1623 began to use the liquation or Seiger process to separate silver from copper. Known in Japanese as *namban-buki*, this method had been invented in Nürnberg in the early fifteenth century, and is said to have been transmitted by a Portuguese metallurgist to the port of Sakai in 1591.

The previous chapter noted that a gold rush in Hokkaido in the early seventeenth century provided cover for Japanese Christians escaping persecution. Diogo Carvalho (1578–1624) disguised himself as a Japanese miner on a voyage to Hokkaido in 1620 and hid with Christian miners. By the 1630s, mining operations had reached eastern Hokkaido. The placer mining method described by Carvalho started to disrupt salmon runs exploited by the Ainu and was one cause of the 1669 Shakushain war between the Ainu and Japanese colonists.

## Glass

Glass beads were imported to Japan from the Bronze Age. An early workshop for local production is known from the seventh-century Asuka-ike site, but before the early modern period most glass was imported. Over forty examples of European blown glass, including cups and bottles, are known from archaeological sites of the Christian Century. The technique of glass-blowing was introduced to Japan at this time and spread from Nagasaki to Edo over the seventeenth century. The Portuguese word *vidro* ("glass") was borrowed into Japanese as *biidoro*.

## Treponemal Disease

From the sixteenth century, treponemal disease began to spread widely across East Asia. Contemporary observers saw this as a sudden, unprecedented phenomenon. Cases in southern China began around 1505. Korean scholar Yi Soo K'wang (1563–1628) wrote about a disease named ch'ŏnp'och'ang, which "Considering the medical literature of our country...originated from China between 1506 and 1521. China did not have this kind of disease in the past. It must have been transmitted from the western world." A later text by Hong Man-seon (1643–1715) described ch'ŏnp'och'ang in terms unmistakable for venereal syphilis. The arrival of syphilis in Japan is usually dated to 1512 when it was reported by a doctor in Kyoto. A year later, syphilis was mentioned in the Myōhōji-ki, a temple record from Yamanashi. A second wave of the disease reached Japan in 1563–64. The Japanese considered southern China to be the source of the first infections.

The sudden spread of treponematosis in East Asia has parallels with Europe, where it also appeared to contemporaries as an epidemic without medical precedent. While the evidence is still sparse and localized, recent research has identified a number of earlier cases of treponemal disease in Europe and the Middle East dating back to at least the sixth century AD and perhaps even a millennium before that. It is now clear that the disease was present long before Columbus, even if there was an increase in cases from the turn of the sixteenth century. In East Asia the situation is less certain. As far as I am aware, there is no accepted skeletal or historical evidence of treponematosis from China, Korea or Japan prior to the beginning of the sixteenth century. Japan has a long tradition of research in physical anthropology and possible skeletal traces of syphilis were described on an Ainu skeleton as early as 1894, one of the first such reports from anywhere in the world. In 1963, Hisashi Suzuki reported three skulls with cranial lesions typical of syphilis from Kajibashi in central Tokyo. While he assigned these remains to the Muromachi period (1336–1573), they were recovered without any recorded archaeological context. In the 1980s, Takao Suzuki analyzed 923 skulls from early modern Edo for evidence of syphilis. His study reported fifty "demonstrable" cases with a further twenty-three "possible" and sixteen "questionable" examples. Suzuki estimated a prevalence of *tertiary* syphilis amongst adults in Edo at between 3.9 and 6.9 per cent, suggesting the surprising conclusion that over half of the adult population of that city was infected with the disease.

Suzuki found higher rates of syphilitic lesions at cemeteries for commoners. He claimed that people of the warrior class were well-educated and self-disciplined, and would thus naturally remain monogamous and "control their sexual passions." By contrast, "the majority of the less-educated or more humble people might not be so continent of their sexual desires." This would point to a difference from medieval Europe where syphilis was especially associated with courtly society. Despite his moralistic tone, Suzuki's interpretation assumes that prostitution was widespread and available even to the lower classes in Edo.

During archaeological fieldwork I conducted at the Nagabaka site on Miyako Island in the southern Ryukyus, we identified skeletal lesions consistent with yaws (*Treponema pallidum pertenue*) from a comingled cemetery dating to the seventeenth to nineteenth centuries.[16] While our identification requires further support from DNA, it suggests the spread of two varieties of treponematosis in Japan from the sixteenth century onwards. This seems to mirror recent DNA studies showing both syphilis and yaws in early modern northern Europe. Clinical research in the Middle East in the 1950s had concluded that while syphilis was found mainly in cities, where prostitution was more easily available, milder forms of treponemal disease were associated with childhood infections spread through skin contact during play. The lack

---

16 Mauricio Hernandez and Mark Hudson, "Diagnosis and Evaluation of Causative Factors for the Presence of Endemic Treponemal Disease in a Japanese Sub Tropical Island Population from the Tokugawa period," *International Journal of Paleopathology* 10 (2015): 16–25.

of historical records of yaws in Okinawa or Japan suggests that syndrome was rare in the archipelago, perhaps because standards of personal hygiene were high. In turn, however, that probably increased the prevalence of the more severe form of venereal syphilis.

Was treponemal disease absent from Japan prior to the sixteenth century, or are we missing relevant cases in the skeletal and documentary records? The disease most often mistaken for syphilis by palaeopathologists is leprosy. The first record of leprosy in Japan is thought to date to the eighth century but skeletal examples are rare or absent before the early modern period, even though the disease is known from medieval written sources. On present evidence, therefore, it seems likely that treponemal disease first reached Japan in the early sixteenth century.

The first wave of syphilis in Japan, dated to 1512, cannot be directly attributed to Europeans and must have been transmitted by Chinese or other merchants, or else by Japanese returning from the mainland, although the timing certainly suggests new global connectivities played a role. The role of Europeans in the second wave (1563–1564) is unclear. As in Europe, syphilis and leprosy were associated with social stigma in Japan. In 1557, Luís d'Almeida set up a hospital in Funai that cared for lepers and syphilitics, marking the first introduction of European medicine to Japan. By 1600, a Jesuit hospital at Nagasaki had a ward for lepers. Notwithstanding the popularity of these institutions, the Society of Jesus decided to exclude lepers and anyone suffering from venereal disease since these were so repulsive (*asquerosos*) to the Japanese. The Franciscans, more open to caring for people with these stigmatized diseases, were criticized by the Jesuits as congregating a "poxy rabble" around them. During the period of persecutions, however, leper huts became one hiding place for priests. At the end of our Century, Christian lepers and beggars from across Japan were rounded up and brought to Nagasaki, from where two boats were sent to Manila with 130 lepers on board in 1632.

While discussing hygiene and medical matters, a brief mention of soap can be made. Soap made of fat and ashes boiled together is known from the Bronze Age, but remained a luxury throughout the Middle Ages. In Japan a soap-like substance has been reported from the eighth-century Shōsōin treasure house in Nara. During the Christian Century, soap introduced by Europeans became more widespread in Japan, though to what extent it was manufactured there is unclear. The earliest documentary mention of soap in Japan dates from 1593 when a samurai records he purchased two bars in Nagasaki.[17] The Japanese word *shabon* ("soap," now archaic) was borrowed from Spanish or Portuguese.

## Christianity and the "Culture Wars" of Late Medieval Japan

The Christian Century saw inventive uses of culture to promote social goals. These "culture wars" were of three types. First, Europeans used art and books to explain both the Christian faith and differences between the nations trading in Japan. Second, the Society of Jesus used Japanese converts as ambassadors for Japanese culture to garner support for their mission in Europe. Finally, the military power wielded by Japanese barons was mirrored by their close attention to social etiquette and fashion.

When Francis Xavier reached Kagoshima in 1549, he brought two oil paintings of the Virgin Mary as a means to explain his faith. The Japanese displayed great interest in European art, which immediately became popular in Japan. Christian art of high quality was produced by Japanese painters after the Jesuits opened a painting school in Nagasaki in 1583 led by Neapolitan Giovanni Colla (1539–1636). Colla, known also as Niccolò, worked in Japan for three decades until the missionaries were expelled in 1614. Japanese pupils copied the European style with such skill that, according to Fróis, "many of the Fathers and Brothers cannot distinguish

---

**17** Reinier Hesselink, "*I go shopping in Christian Nagasaki*: Entries from the Diary of a Mito Samurai, Ōwada Shigekiyo (1593)," *Bulletin of Portuguese/Japanese Studies*, 2nd series, 1 (2015): 27–45.

which are their paintings and which are the paintings done in Rome." Although missionaries appealed to Japanese understandings of religious doctrine, they acknowledged the power of images and ritual. Gnecchi-Soldo Organtino explained in 1577 that, "Our experience shows that we will receive Japanese converts by millions, if we can promote the worship of Deus by ritual. If we have choirs and musical instruments such as organs, all the people in Miyako and Sakai will undoubtedly become Kirishitan within a year.'" Organtino concluded that "In serving the Truth, ritual is the most effective method."[18] In addition to religious works, European painting also began to influence Japanese art with respect to technique (especially the use of perspective), colour, and genre.

The English were keenly aware of the value of gift diplomacy in their attempts to open trade. Their first voyage, which reached Kyushu in 1613, carried a variety of presents including a silver-gilt telescope. Timon Screech has argued that the telescope was a deeply symbolic gift, a critique of the political intrigues of the Jesuits yet also a way of placing the English at the forefront of scientific research. A third English voyage, dispatched in 1614, was loaded with almost a hundred oil paintings. John Saris, captain of the first expedition, had described how during a visit to his ship in Hirado by ladies "of the better sort," they had mistaken the Venus depicted on a painting in his cabin for the Virgin Mary. Though apparently not Christians themselves, they began to "worship" the image. Such paintings offered the English a chance to explain how their country differed theologically from the Roman Catholic nations.

Aware of the role of printing in the spread of Protestantism, the Jesuits brought a hand press to Nagasaki in 1590. Although woodblock printing had long been used in Japan, this was the first use there of moveable metal type. Until it was forced to close in 1614, around one hundred books were published, more than thirty of which still exist. During its last decade, the press was often moved between secret locations.

---

**18** Higashibaba, *Christianity in Early Modern Japan*, 102.

Some texts were printed in Japanese using the Roman script, a style of writing also used for handwritten communications by Japanese converts, often to maintain secrecy.

Two embassies by Japanese Christians to Catholic Europe are conventionally labelled by the reign eras when they occurred: the Tenshō (in Europe 1584–86) and the Keichō (1614–16). Comprised of four teenage boys, the Tenshō legation travelled from Portugal to Spain and Italy. Everywhere they travelled, the boys were warmly welcomed and given food and gifts. In Rome they met Pope Gregory, who died three weeks after their first audience. Three of the Japanese boys were then given important roles in the coronation Mass of the new Pope Sixtus V, the fourth unable to participate due to sickness. Michael Cooper noted three main objectives behind the legation: to obtain financial support for the Japan mission, to make Europe better known in Japan, and to maintain the Jesuit monopoly on missionary work in Japan. On the first point, a Dominican friar in Japan later complained how the Jesuits had claimed the boys came from great families only "to get money for their mission." With respect to the third objective, Valignano believed that mendicant friars, many of whom had worked in South America or the Philippines, would set back his policy of accommodation to Japanese culture, perhaps even introducing a "conquistador" attitude. The embassy indubitably generated considerable interest in Europe: by the end of the sixteenth century, some seventy publications in European languages provided accounts of the legation and its background.

The Keichō Embassy was headed by Hasekura Tsunenaga, a samurai of the Sendai domain. Departing Japan in 1613, Hasegawa crossed the Pacific to Mexico before travelling on to Europe, returning by the same route in 1620. Hasekura was baptized in Spain in 1615. Visiting Rome later that year, he met Pope Paul V. Some members of Hasegawa's large Japanese retinue may have remained in Spain but the others returned to a country where persecution of Christianity had started in earnest, although the fate of Hasegawa himself is unclear. Due to its timing, the long-term diplomatic and trading impacts of the Keichō Embassy were minimal. As with the previous Tenshō legation, however, the Japanese visitors aroused considerable interest in Europe.

On the Japanese side, curiosity soon overcame consternation and Iberia became "fashionable." A series of genre paintings on folding screens depicted Europeans, Indians, Africans and Native Americans interacting with Japanese people in ports and towns. Ronald Toby has emphasized that while foreigners had always been common visitors to Japan, they had previously been "invisible"; that is, they had not been depicted in artistic works in the context of the Japanese everyday. The "Iberian irruption" meant that Koreans, Manchus, and Ryukyuans were also depicted as distinct from "Chinese" for the first time.[19] Meanwhile, the material trappings of Christianity became popular, and even non-believers sometimes wore crosses and rosaries. Nobunaga had a large wardrobe of *namban* garments and Hideyoshi wore a rosary. A 1594 letter by Francisco Pasio noted that:

> [Hideyoshi] has become so enamoured of Portuguese dress and costume that he and his retainers frequently wear this apparel, as do all the other lords of Japan, even the gentiles, with rosaries of driftwood on the breast...and with a crucifix at their side...; some of them are so curious that they learn by rote the litanies of *Pater Noster* and *Ave Maria* and go along praying in the streets, not in mockery or scorn... but simply for gallantry, or because they think it is a good thing and one which will help them to achieve prosperity in worldly things.[20]

A depiction of Izumo-no-Okuni (ca. 1572–ca. 1613), one of the founders of *kabuki* theatre, shows her wearing a rosary and cross while performing. A screen showing the 1604 commemoration of the seventh anniversary of Hideyoshi's death includes

---

**19** Toby, *Engaging the Other*, 78–79.

**20** Boxer, *Christian Century*, 207–8. For Nobunaga, see Toby, *Engaging the Other*, 22, 129–32. Toby notes that Hideyoshi also enjoyed dressing as a Chinese emperor.

Japanese dancers wearing *namban* clothes.[21] Exotic dress provided Hideyoshi—who had been born a peasant—with a cultural capital that emphasized both his position outside the traditional status system and his role in controlling the new outsiders. Tailors in Nagasaki were forced to work around the clock in order to satisfy the demand for Iberian-style clothing. Hideyoshi even had a European-style bed made for himself.

Dress was an important though under-studied category of cultural exchange during the Christian Century. Different textiles lead themselves to different styles of clothing and embodiment. In the Bronze Age, archaeologists have discussed how wool would have created new "body cultures" in contrast to the older plant fibres. Late medieval and Renaissance Europe saw growing use of buttons. The Portuguese word *botão* was quickly borrowed into Japanese as *botan*, though buttons on clothing were rarely used in Japan until the nineteenth century. In Europe, the Japanese robes worn by the boys of the Tenshō embassy were much admired and sometimes copied.

The Counter-Reformation was supported in Asia by local production of religious objects. In 1590, the Dominican bishop of Manila, Domingo de Salazar, extolled the "marvellous things" made by Chinese craftsmen there, writing "I think that nothing more perfect could be produced than some of their ivory statues which I have seen." The ivory itself came from Africa, while some of the objects manufactured in Manila were exported on to Mexico, Peru, and even Europe. A collection of Spanish-Philippine ivories can be seen in the church of Santa María de Mediavilla in Median de Rioseco, Spain. Paintings of the Madonna of the Snows were made by indigenous artists from Mexico to India, and a Japanese example dating to around the first decade of the seventeenth century is exhibited in the Twenty-Six Martyrs' Museum in Nagasaki. Lacquered wooden furniture exported from Japan in the early seventeenth century included items for religious devotion, such as lecterns and crosses.

---

**21** Illustrated in Toby, *Engaging the Other*, 115.

Ceramics were another category of material culture with great social significance. Valignano was astonished by the Japanese interest in old pots. "The King of Bungo," he wrote, "once showed me a small earthenware [tea] caddy for which, in all truth, we would have no other use than to put it in a bird's cage as a drinking trough; nevertheless, he had paid 9000 silver taels for it." Japanese merchants made trips to the Philippines to obtain Sung dynasty tea jars. Tea bowls were also imported from Korea to Japan, where they were called Koryŏ bowls even though most were made in the later Chosŏn dynasty. Japanese interest in old Chinese and Korean ceramics was later matched by the acquisition of contemporary European wares, especially tin-glazed pots. Originating in the Hispano-Moresque wares of al-Andalus, production of *majolica* pottery spread to Italy, then north to Holland and England in the sixteenth century, later becoming known as Delftware. Around thirty pieces of such pottery have been excavated from Japan. Tokugawa Hidetada was buried in 1632 with a tin-glazed *albarello*. Used as medicine jars in Europe, polychrome cylindrical *albarelli* with leaf motifs account for the majority of this type of ceramic discovered from early modern Japan. Archaeologist Keiko Matsumoto notes that, in contrast to Europe, Japanese examples were glazed on the inside as well as the outside. She suggests that some of these vessels were produced as special orders for use in the tea ceremony.

Although archaeological examples in Japan are relatively rare, large quantities of tin-glazed pottery were shipped from Europe in the seventeenth century. English East India Company records show that eighteen crates of these "gallipots" were sent in 1614. When the English closed their Japanese venture in 1623, their Hirado warehouse still had 2,000 unsold gallipots. Timon Screech argues that the *albarello* buried with Hidetada may have derived from the Montague Close kiln in London, which opened in 1571. However, based on analyses of the form, technique of manufacture and decorative designs, Matsumoto proposes that the Japanese finds are Dutch, probably from Amsterdam.

Perhaps the most controversial point of connection between Japanese culture and the Christian Century is the tea ceremony. First introduced to Japan in the eighth century, tea was increasingly consumed by all social classes by the late medieval period. Developing from the fifteenth century, the tea ceremony became popular amongst the aristocracy in the sixteenth. A speculative literature has proposed similarities between the tea ceremony and eucharistic liturgy: in both cases the ritual involves raising the container to head height as a mark of respect and wiping the bowl after each drink with a white cloth. Such ideas will seem outlandish to some readers and there is no direct supporting evidence, yet it is difficult to completely exclude such a link. We know that the Jesuits understood the importance of tea in Japanese culture; implements for the tea ceremony were kept at hand at Jesuit buildings to entertain important guests. At the very least, we can conclude that the culture of tea formed a peaceful "middle ground" between Europe and Japan during our Century.

Finally, we can briefly mention the numerous European loanwords borrowed into Japanese. Portuguese loans include *pan* ("bread"), *tabako* ("tobacco"), *kappa* (*capa*, "raincoat"), *karuta* ("playing cards"), *kompeito* (*confeito*, confit or sweets), *jōro* (*jarro*, "jug"), and *bateren* (*padre*, "holy father"). One of the more unusual loans is *miira*, meaning a mummified body. This derived from the Portuguese word for myrrh (*mirra*) and seems to have involved a confusion between the latter substance and the mummified human body parts that were traded by Europeans as medicine.[22]

## Vast, Cold, and Sheepless? Limits to Trade in the Christian Century

The English East India Company, established in 1600, was initially interested in spices from Southeast Asia, but in 1611

---

**22** On mummified remains as medicine, see Michael Kinski, "*Materia Medica* in Edo Period: The Case of *Mummy*. Takai Ranzan's *Shokuji kai*, Part Two," *Japonica Humboldtiana* 9 (2005): 55–170.

a fleet of ships under John Saris sailed for Japan in the hope of obtaining silver, silk, and lacquerware. The main commodity offered in exchange was England's most famous product, wool. Winters in Japan can be extremely cold, a condition not helped in the seventeenth century by the cooler temperatures of the Little Ice Age, nor by the rampant deforestation of the Warring States. Fróis wrote that Kyoto suffered from a lack of firewood due to forest clearance. In an early letter, Xavier requested clothes made of Portuguese wool, "for here we are dying of cold." All of this seemed to make Japan a perfect market for wool. Screech speculates that the promise of a "vast, cold and sheepless" Japan emboldened King James in 1614 to enact the Cockayne Scheme whereby English cloth was to be exported in a finished condition, a measure that quickly led to a Dutch boycott since the cloth had previously been dyed and finished in the Netherlands. Sheep had reached northern China as early as the fifth millennium BC, but were not raised in Japan in any numbers until the twentieth century. Some sheep may have been imported into European enclaves but, unlike goats, were not widely adopted by the Japanese.

Eleven days after Saris's ship the *Clove* arrived back in London, George Abbot, Archbishop of Canterbury and brother of the deputy-governor of the East India Company, wrote a letter to his hometown of Guilford proposing it turn itself into a production centre of broadcloth for the Japanese market. Abbot sent £100 to be distributed to weavers who were prepared to change their looms for the new endeavour. In 1599 Abbot had published *A Brief Description of the Whole World* in which he claimed English wool was "renowned over a great part of the earth." Despite this, English dreams of a lasting trading relationship with Japan were not realized. Wool did not become a popular commodity in Japan and the last English trading post closed in 1623. The fact that wool was subject to rotting on long sea journeys is noted by Screech. Wool was also difficult to keep clean; unlike cotton, it cannot be boiled and tended to harbour lice. Imported wool was sometimes used for military clothing and dyed red with American cochineal. Unlike Europe, however, cochineal dyes were rare in early modern Japan, perhaps because lac, an insect dye produced in Southeast Asia, was less expensive.

Textile production in Japan was undergoing a major transformation at the time of the Christian Century as cotton became widely used. The first record of cotton in Japan dates to 799, but it was not cultivated there until the late fifteenth century. By the late sixteenth century, cotton was being grown in the Kanto region. Rodrigues wrote that the use of cotton "has greatly increased since we went to Japan." Aside from clothing, cotton was also used for musket wicks and sails.

## Conclusions

While the spread of Christianity in late medieval Japan is often discussed in terms of a clash of civilizations, this chapter highlighted the archipelago's entangled cultural relationships with Europe. We can continue to debate the appropriateness of the label "Christian Century," yet social and ecological histories show how Japan became impacted by new global connectivities. As in Europe, New World crops were met with a mixture of resistance and receptivity but enhanced the diversity and resilience of Japanese foodways. Iberian cuisine influenced Japan, especially in the growing popularity of eggs and sugar. The spread of treponemal disease across Japan reflected new global links even if it was not initially introduced through European contact. Japanese responses to the encounter with Europe were diverse yet, outside of religion, the country was transformed by a range of entanglements—agricultural, culinary, artistic, linguistic, scientific, and epidemiological. Although the Tokugawa "closing" of the country made European influences more fraught, the global entanglements of the Christian Century continued to impact early modern Japan.

Chapter 5

# Re-Thinking the Christian Century: Global Contexts, Local Afterlives

This book has explored European impacts on late medieval Japan, a task made difficult by the confluence of several strong currents in Japanese historiography. The trend to see Japan "on its own terms"—to emphasize the independent historical evolution of the nation—is perhaps the fastest-flowing of those currents. In this view, Japan developed towards a similar goal to the West (modernity), yet that endpoint was achieved *without* colonial control. Early modern Japan thus not only helps assuage the sins of European colonialism but, because the country was supposedly isolated, also provides a model for environmental sustainability and wise use of limited resources. This romanticized view of Japan's traditional "harmony" with nature has been invoked in numerous writings, including Jared Diamond's *Collapse*.

A frequent critique of the Christian Century relegates it to a Eurocentric conceit breaking up the natural continuity of Japanese history where, despite damage to the body politic during the Warring States' conflicts, the realm was saved by the heroic efforts of the three great hegemons. Against this background, Europeans are seen as the most unpredictable threat to Japanese unity. I have argued here that this overestimates the role of potential European violence—constructed as fanatical and illegitimate—in contrast to the "rational" and necessary violence of the hegemons.

Another historical current flows from the significant differences between Western views of Japan in the sixteenth and nineteenth centuries. The Jesuits believed that Christianity was superior to any of the beliefs found in Japan, even if they recognized a certain sophistication in Buddhist theology. But Europeans in the Christian Century did not as a whole assume that European *civilization* was more advanced than that of Japan. By the nineteenth century, things had changed. American naval Commodore Matthew Perry saw Japan as "the youngest sister in the circle of commercial nations," requiring "older kindly" countries to "take her by the hand" and "aid her tottering steps." Similar comments were made by Douglas MacArthur, commander of the American Occupation after the Second World War. European accounts of Japan during the Christian Century had their own prejudices but accepted the country as one of the most mature civilizations of Eurasia. For their part, Japanese élites initially looked down on the "Southern Barbarians" but benefited from their trade and quickly came to adopt a range of Iberian goods and customs.

## Japan's Crypto-Christians: From Hidden Practice to World Heritage

When missionaries of the Société des missions étrangères de Paris were allowed into Japan in 1859, they began to hear rumours of underground "Hidden Christians." These crypto-Christians had maintained their beliefs in the face of considerable danger for over two centuries, yet their practices were regarded as mere superstitions by the French priests. For the Catholic Church of the nineteenth century, the possibility of a native Christianity was denied; the hidden practices were the regrettable result of apostasy. Yet as many as 35,000 crypto-Christians refused to rejoin the Church, believing that they were keeping the true faith of their ancestors and expressing dismay at the condescending attitudes of nineteenth-century Westerners.

In Japanese, a distinction is made between *Sempuku Kirishitan* ("Secret Christians"), used until 1873 when the ban on Christianity was removed, and *Kakure Kirishitan* ("Hidden Christians") after that date. Here I use the term "crypto-Christians," prefixed by "former" when referring to events after 1873. As many as 150,000 Christians went underground during the persecutions of the early seventeenth century. In 1657, long after direct persecutions had finished, 600 Christians were discovered and arrested at Ōmura near Nagasaki. Almost five hundred of these were executed or died in prison, while the remainder were forced to apostatize. In 1664–1667, another 2,000 Christians were arrested near Nagoya, not previously known as a centre of the faith. In the nineteenth century, hidden Christian communities were found all over Japan, including in the cities of Kyoto and Edo, although the groups of the coasts and islands of northwest Kyushu have been studied most.

Crypto-Christians transmitted their beliefs through prayers (*orasho*, from Latin *oratio*) and secret lay confraternities. Without churches, prayers were made inside homes or were directed at places where their ancestors had been martyred or at scared islands or mountains. Small crucifixes made of paper could be eaten to avoid discovery. Fasts (*zejun* from Portuguese *jejum*) were performed. Sacred objects, known as *nandogami* ("closet *kami*") or *osugata* (a translation of Portuguese *imagem*), were often visibly indistinguishable from Buddhist or folk items. The Tokugawa Inquisition noted that believers sometimes engraved tiny *imagem* on sword pommels. Small statues of the Buddhist Kannon Goddess of Mercy were associated with the Virgin Mary. Crypto-Christians made straw whips called *otenpesha* (from Portuguese *penitencia* with the honorific prefix *o*-); no longer used for flagellation, these became similar to Shinto *gohei* wands to drive out evil spirits. A special prayer was recited before visits to Buddhist temples or *e-fumi* (forced trampling on sacred images). There was also some degree of toleration by local lords. For example, thousands of crypto-Christians were moved from Ōmura to the Gotō Islands as agricultural settlers by Gotō Moriyuki (1752–1809). The fact that none of these people were exposed as Christians suggests connivance by the authorities involved.[1]

---

1 Peter Nosco, "Secrecy and the Transmission of Tradition: Issues

Most scholars of Japanese crypto-Christians have understood them in terms of syncretic folk practices, suggesting that doctrinal "flexibility" made it easier to survive persecution. Yet hidden religious practices were hardly restricted to Japan in the early modern period. One comparable example from Europe would be the Protestants of the Cévennes in southern France who, after Louis XIV revoked the Edict of Nantes in 1685, practised their faith in secret locations, described by one contemporary as "sometimes in Woods, and at other times in Caves, and Rocks, and Dens of the Earth." They read literature banned in France and developed a faith based on landscape. Comparisons between such examples of underground Christians would be instructive but, to my knowledge, have not been systematically attempted.

In 2007, the Japanese government added "Churches and Christian Sites in Nagasaki" to the UNESCO World Heritage Tentative List. Nine years later this application was withdrawn and replaced by a new one titled "Hidden Christian Sites in the Nagasaki Region." It was this new application that was successfully inscribed as World Heritage in 2018. The twelve components of the property include villages and sacred places, the remains of Hara castle (besieged during the Shimabara revolt), and Ōura basilica in Nagasaki. Tinka Delakorda Kawashima has analysed how the Japanese government changed its original focus on the built heritage of churches to one centred on a cultural landscape. This shift follows a recent trend in heritage management towards consideration of lived environments. Nevertheless, Kawashima notes how the application worked to exclude former crypto-Christians still living in the area. The final executive summary continues this approach, assessing the World Heritage value in the past tense as follows: "the property represents how the Christian communities survived in the midst of the conventional society and its religions, gradually transforming and ultimately ending their religious traditions and being assimilated into modern society after the prohibition was lifted."[2]

## The Seed of the Old Martyrs: Japan on the Jesuit Stage

Jesuit writings on Japan had an enormous impact in Europe, where they stimulated representations of the country in a wide range of media, including books, plays, pictures, even music.[3] From a European perspective, the century 1543–1639 had a certain unity in the availability of first-hand information about Japan. After 1640, such information became more limited, though an exception was the writings of Engelbert Kaempfer (1651–1716), a German physician who worked for the Dutch at Nagasaki. Counter-Reformation Europe saw Japan as a "distant mirror" of the struggles and advances of the faith, not least for recusant Catholics in England.[4] The Japanese martyrs were particularly important in this respect since they counterbalanced Protestant narratives of persecution, in addition to suggesting parallels with the early Church. The prologue to the 1638 play *Christianomachia Iaponensis*

---

**2** Government of Japan, *Executive Summary: Hidden Christian Sites in the Nagasaki Region*, https://whc.unesco.org/en/list/1495/documents/, 6.

**3** An oratorio titled *La conversion alla santa fede del re di Bungo giaponese* and dealing with the "king of Bungo" (Ōtomo Yoshishige) was performed near Bologna in 1703; see Makoto H. Takao, "Francis Xavier at the court of Ōtomo Yoshishige," *Journal of Jesuit Studies* 3 (2016): 451–74.

**4** Liam M. Brockey and Jurgis S. A. Elisonas, "The Tragedy of Quabacondono: An Elizabethan Account of the Last Days of Toyotomi Hideyoshi," *Monumenta Nipponica* 76 (2021): 1–68. The Jesuit experience in Japan also influenced the organization of missions in the Americas; see Takao Abé, *The Jesuit Mission to New France: A New Interpretation in the Light of the Earlier Jesuit Experience in Japan* (Leiden: Brill, 2011).

("Battle of the Japanese Christians") explains how the Church rejoices that the "seed of the old martyrs grows" in foreign countries such as Japan, in opposition to enemies both old (the Devil) and new ("Queen Elizabeth of England together with Heresy").

Franciscans were the first to employ the 1597 execution of the "Twenty-six Martyrs of Nagasaki" for propaganda purposes. The story of the martyrs reached Mexico where it was depicted on an early seventeenth-century fresco in the cathedral of Cuernavaca. The Society of Jesus soon took up the same theme. Around 650 Jesuit educational plays dealing with Japan are known, mostly from the seventeenth century, although Japanese themes continued to be popular until the 1773 suppression of the Society. Written in Neo-Latin, the allegorical plays were performed at Jesuit institutions from Lithuania to Ireland. Only a few actual plays exist as hand-written manuscripts, but printed playbills are more common. While it is difficult to evaluate the broader social impact of these plays beyond Jesuit circles, their spirited inclusion of Japanese themes probably had a not insignificant impact on a Baroque Europe eager for news of Catholic success in the East.

## Did Premodern Japan Have Religions?

The deep engagement of many Japanese converts with Christianity encourages a re-evaluation of recent claims that the whole concept of "religion" was a colonial construct forced on Japan in the nineteenth century. It cannot be questioned that Western imperialism generated new ways of classifying the world and that religion became a key element in Orientalist discourse in the nineteenth century. Understandings of religion changed as it became subject to academic inquiry. From this background, discussed by Tomoko Masuzawa in *The Invention of World Religions*, several studies have looked at Japan. Timothy Fitzgerald's *The Ideology of Religious Studies* has been widely critiqued by Japan specialists, who have accused the author of the same cultural essentialism he claims to be deconstructing. Jason Josephson's *The Invention of Religion in Japan* is the more important work, yet unconvincing regarding the Christian Century. Josephson argues Christianity was seen as a Japanese heresy, not a separate religion. While anti-Christian directives did indeed make that claim, Josephson is in effect seeing Christianity *like a state*. For Tokugawa authorities, a foreign religion was far more dangerous than a Japanese heresy; classification under the latter label buttressed the impression the state was still in control, while deliberately ignoring the fact that Christianity was clearly *not* Japanese in origin.

Valignano believed the Japanese had a natural inclination to religion, making them open to Christianity. In contrast, some historians have emphasized the conditional or "worldly" aspects of conversion in late medieval Japan. Ōtomo Sōrin is said to have converted to obtain cannon; the faith of other barons is frequently seen as shallow or provisional. For instance, Ōmura Sumitada Bartolomeu was a key supporter of Christianity in Nagasaki but later took the tonsure in Shingon Buddhism. While it was customary for soldiers to adopt a Buddhist role upon retirement, Sumitada/Bartolomeu's combination is regarded by some as symbolic of the ambiguous status of Christianity in Japan, demonstrating the resilience of "Eastern thought" and, at the same time, the emerging secular, hence modern, nature of Tokugawa society. It was precisely this combination—the West as secular and modern, the East as superstitious and traditional—that characterized the growing field of "world religions" in the nineteenth century. Even if the modern generic word for religion (*shūkyō*) only became common in the nineteenth century, it is hard to read the events of the Christian Century and its aftermath through the assumption that the Japanese had no concept of religion.

During their encounter in the late sixteenth century, Europeans and Japanese both realized that religious differences existed between them, but they did not assume those differences represented a previously unknown domain of human behaviour. At first, there was a search for similarities and overlap between Christianity and Buddhism. How the Jesuit mission gradually came to understand the religious differences presented by Buddhism is a topic of considerable interest. While it might be an exaggeration to say there was real dialogue between the faiths, the Society of Jesus invested considerable effort in explication of the diverse *seitas gentílicas* (gentile sects) of Japan.[5] The eventual response of Japan's rulers to growing Iberian influence in the archipelago was to utilize native religious traditions. The Tokugawa regime attempted to curtail the power of autonomous religious institutions in favour of a new orthopraxy. From 1664, a temple certification system forced all Japanese to register as Buddhists, though some domain lords attempted to institute registration based on Shinto shrines.

A division between religion and secularism has been proposed as another Western colonial export but, as mentioned already, several historians posit a shift to a more "worldly" society in early modern Japan. The enforced new orthopraxy made affiliation to Buddhist temples a question of "political obligation rather than religious conviction," leading to the "general lethargy and uncreativeness of Buddhism in the Tokugawa Period."[6] In broad outline, Tokugawa secularism mirrors the trend found in early modern Europe, an argument made by Bellah almost seventy years ago. The history of secularism in both Europe and Japan is a hotly-debated topic. Previous writings by Bellah and others have limited their focus to the Tokugawa period, ignoring the preceding Christian Century via the (unstated) assumption that Tokugawa policies were a "rational" response to the "irrational" anti-modern excesses of Catholicism. Following recent research in Europe, however, there is a need to consider how the religious pluralism of late medieval Japan, which included Christianity, generated a shifting relationship between religion and the secular.

---

**5** Joan-Pau Rubiés, "Real and Imaginary Dialogues in the Jesuit Mission of Sixteenth-Century Japan," *Journal of the Economic and Social History of the Orient* 55 (2012): 447–94.

**6** Robert Bellah, *Tokugawa Religion: The Cultural Roots of Modern Japan* (New York: Free, 1985), 51.

## A Changed World: Japan, Global History, and the Christian Century

As mentioned in the Preface, my work on the period considered here began with an interest in premodern globalization. While the history of the Japanese Islands is often discussed in terms of essential isolation reluctantly broken up by short phases of external contact, even those stages of unambiguous connectivity are frequently contested. The Christian Century was Japan's first global moment. Japanese envoys, monks, and traders had long been active across East and Southeast Asia, but Japanese people now reached Europe for the first time; Japanese mercenaries were employed in Mexico; some Japanese slaves, and a smaller number of free individuals, ended up in Iberian imperial cities, including Goa, Lima, Lisbon, and Seville. In part because there are few historical sources that directly record the experiences of these travellers, historical writing since the 1970s has re-centred Japan away from Europe and global links. On one level this can be understood as a reaction to the label "Christian Century," which perhaps inevitably suggests a historical scaffolding or even unity revolving around Europe. As I have shown, however, any such unity was short-lived and born of diversity. If globalization in Japanese history is often approached in terms of contact and ensuing *conflict* between two mutually exclusive modes of thought—Japanese (or "Eastern") and "Western"—an attempt has been made here to portray cultural exchange between Europe and Japan as a complex process, an entangled web rather than a clash of civilizations. Again, the objection can be raised that the term "Christian Century" does not encompass such complexities. A hybrid label such as "Ibero-Japanese Century" might be more appropriate, but I have argued that Christianity itself can be considered as an important element of the very hybridity of the period.

While there are significant historiographic barriers to understanding the Christian Century, many key questions in Japanese history are connected to interpretations of that era. What was the relationship between isolation and globalization? Do the most fundamental and "authentic" elements of Japanese culture stem from periods of isolation rather than episodes of outside contact? How did isolation affect the development of modernity in Japan? It is clear that even during times of relative isolation, Japan still experienced a broad range of cross-border processes, including commercial exchange, the spread of religious and scholastic ideas, and of course epidemic disease. From the Bronze Age to the seventeenth century, decentralized maritime and peasant modes of production remained important in the archipelago despite competing tributary and feudal modes. Maritime traders maintained a network of links across East and Southeast Asia. The unification of Japan at the end of the sixteenth century was achieved by fierce opposition to any type of local autonomy—economic, religious, or otherwise—through what Amino called "agrarian fundamentalism." The agrarian fundamentalist paradigm has come to dominate writings on early modern Japan. The increased consumption of global goods is played down in favour of a model that valorizes isolation and embeddedness in a circular economy. This model of Tokugawa Japan as "spaceship earth" is even proposed to hold lessons for *global* sustainability. However, the broader history of consumption is ignored in such imaginings. If Europe experienced a "consumer revolution" in the eighteenth century, a comparable trend was found in Japan. Although demand in Japan was sometimes met by local production of global goods such as sugar and silk, Japan's early modern consumer revolution was not curtailed by the isolationist policies of the Tokugawa government.

The Christian Century forced Japan to confront new worlds beyond eastern Asia. There had been some awareness of people from western Eurasia and coastal Africa (though not from the Americas) before the sixteenth century, but the "Iberian irruption" made those foreigners a visible part of the social fabric. The social changes that affected Japan during the Christian Century match many of the trends proposed in research on globalization, such as Justin Jenning's *Globalizations in the Ancient World* (2011). *Time-space compression* generated a "shrinking" world where previously distant things seemed closer and more connected to everyday experience. *Deterritorialization* meant the significance of a place appeared abstracted from "fixed" local content, a change expressed in contemporary *namban* art such as that reproduced on the cover of this book. Both *cultural homogenization* and *heterogeneity* characterized late medieval Japan's response to Europe and global trade. *Vulnerability* and the *re-embedding of local culture* formed key elements of social and political responses in the seventeenth century.

In both Japan and Europe, the sixteenth and seventeenth centuries were a time of the shifting politics of nation-building; the nation was re-formulated through the lens of global or globalizing processes. As a result, Europe and Japan both underwent radical re-evaluations of their place in the world. For Catholic Europe, Japan seemed to offer the opportunity to establish a new community of believers on the far side of the world and thus reclaim some of the losses of the Protestant Reformation. Despite striking cultural differences, there was much about Japanese society that felt familiar. If Native Americans presented a deep challenge with respect to their social equality, Japan appeared refreshingly normal in its inequalities. Some Jesuits even complained that the biggest problem in Japan (aside from sodomy) was that the people did not always obey their lords. José de Acosta placed the Japanese in his first level of peoples who possessed a similar degree of civilization to Europeans and should be converted through reason rather than force. As we have seen, the Japanese mission continued to serve as a didactic trope in Jesuit schools well into the eighteenth century. Jesuit successes in Japan were used by the English as propaganda against "Popish intrigue"—as it turned out all too successfully. Aside from trade, which the English found unprofitable after 1623, there was initially little effort invested in inserting Japan within a Protestant world-view. Protestant Europe was less flexible with respect to "converting" Japan than the Catholic south

Japanese historians have acknowledged that major changes occurred during our period, but link those changes with later developments, especially with "modernization," an assumed universal status or destination whereby Japan could sit at the right hand of the United States. Doubts were raised about this trajectory by Japanese scholars as early as the 1950s. Indeed, Japanese capitalism quickly demonstrated that its success was *not* due to "universal," let alone American features. Ezra Vogel's 1979 *Japan as Number One: Lessons for America* turned the equation on its head, but the relationship between "East" and "West" continues to influence the writing of history in/about Japan. A point I have tried to make here is that the Christian Century was a time when the question of universalism was debated and negotiated in surprisingly complex ways. The always-strained East/West dichotomy begins to break down. This was certainly a period of dramatic change, one whose *a*-typical elements are frequently stressed, yet many trends in Japanese history at the time mirror those in other parts of Eurasia—notably political centralization, growing commercialization, and cultural standardization. This argument has been made in detail by Victor Lieberman in his work *Strange Parallels*. Some Japanese scholars have argued for a deeper standardization of Japanese culture than was achieved in Europe during the early modern period, but Mary Berry is sceptical of such claims. She notes that while the polity was integrated, the very process of consolidation generated new diversities of occupation, urban culture, art, clothing, even religion.[7] The Japan of the Christian Century was marked by popular desires to embrace the new. While the Tokugawa state strived to curtail those desires, it was not entirely successful.

One historian has written that "Too much and too little can be made of the Christians and traders who came

---

**7** Victor Lieberman, *Strange Parallels: Southeast Asia in Global Context, c. 800-1830*, 2 vols. (New York: Cambridge University Press, 2003 and 2009); Mary E. Berry, "Was Early Modern Japan Culturally Integrated?" in *Beyond Binary Histories: Re-imagining Eurasia to c. 1830*, ed. Victor Lieberman (Ann Arbor: University of Michigan Press, 1999), 103–37.

to Japan after 1543."[8] *Too much*, because internal political and economic transformations within the archipelago were significant and there is a danger of confusing the colonizing abilities of Europeans in the sixteenth century with those of the nineteenth. Yet *too little*, because the Christian Century saw enormous impacts over many areas of Japanese life—religious, military, political, cultural, and culinary. To attempt another paradoxical but precise coda, we might say that while the main characteristics of both the medieval and early modern eras in Japan owed little to Europe directly, Europe played a key role in the *transition* between those two periods. Andrew Goble proposes three distinct features of Japan's Middles Ages: military violence, social mobility, and overseas contact. The Christian Century saw a climax of those features but they did not derive primarily from European influence. In contrast to the medieval, Mary Berry points to a strong state and penetration of a market economy as defining the early modern in Japan. She notes similarities (and differences) with Europe and other parts of the early modern world.[9] While I am in agreement with these characterizations, I feel we are missing the continuities between them, the social and economic rhythms through which the Christian Century provided the context for the transformation.

Finally, while globalization may sometimes seem an anonymous and deterministic process, Japan's Christian Century offers reflections on the human interactions involved. Writing shortly after his imprisonment by the Japanese army from 1941–1945, Boxer noted that the Century had its own lessons in evil. Yet he also commented on how many ordinary Japanese at the time were open to social interaction with Europeans. While the idea of Europe as "threat" has dominated historical discourse, what is interesting about the period con-

---

**8** George Wilson, *Patriots and Redeemers in Japan: Motives in the Meiji Restoration* (Chicago: University of Chicago Press, 1992), 35.

**9** Goble, "Defining 'Medieval'" and Berry, "Defining 'Early Modern'," in *Japan Emerging: Premodern History to 1850*, ed. Karl Friday (Boulder: Westview, 2012), 32–41 and 42–52.

sidered here is the impact Europeans had in Japan *without* any decisive military advantage. This impact was achieved by the way Europeans, missionaries, and merchants alike, adapted to the opportunities and constraints of late medieval Japan, but also by Japanese interest in what Europe had to offer at a time of conflict and uncertainty. The Christian Century was an age of violence but also one of partnership.

# Further Reading

## Contemporary Sources

Cooper, Michael, ed. *João Rodrigues's Account of Sixteenth-Century Japan* (London: Hakluyt Society, 2001).

> Chapters on history, geography, banquets, printing, and many other topics.

Cooper, Michael. *They Came to Japan: An Anthology of European Reports on Japan (1543-1640)* (Berkeley: University of California Press, 1965).

> A selection of European writings on a range of topics.

Danford, Richard, Robin Gill, and Daniel Reff, eds. and trans. *The First European Description of Japan, 1585: A Critical English-language Edition of "Striking Contrasts in the Customs of Europe and Japan" by Luis Frois, S. J.* (Abingdon: Routledge, 2014).

> A comparison of European and Japanese culture believed to have been written by Jesuit Luís Fróis.

Fróis, Luís. *Historia de Japam*, 5 vols. (Lisbon: Biblioteca Nacional de Lisboa, 1976-1984).

> A key resource, edited and annotated by José Wicki.

Lidin, Olaf G. *Tanegashima: The Arrival of Europe in Japan* (Copenhagen: Nordic Institute of Asian Studies, 2002).

> Explores the earliest Portuguese arrivals on Tanegashima and the first production of firearms. Includes critical translations of contemporary sources such as the *Teppōki*.

San Emeterio, Gonzalo, trans. *Shimabaraki: Una crónica de la rebelión de Shimabara* (Madrid: UAM Ediciones, 2019).

> Annotated Spanish translation of the *Shimabaraki*, a 1640 account of the Shimabara uprising. Includes a long introduction and the original Japanese text with *furigana* readings.

## Japan's First Encounter with Europe

Alonge, Guillaume. *A History of Jesuit Missions in Japan: Evangelization, Miracles and Martyrdom, 1549-1614* (Abingdon: Routledge, 2024).

> A short overview which examines both Japanese responses to Christianity and the rivalry between Jesuits and mendicant orders.

Boxer, C. R. *The Christian Century in Japan, 1549-1650* (Cambridge: Cambridge University Press, 1951).

> The standard introduction to the period remains a key resource.

Cabezas García, Antonio. *El Siglo Ibérico de Japón: La presencia Hispano-Portuguesa en Japón (1543-1643)* (Valladolid: Universidad de Valladolid, 1995).

> A single-volume history of the period that provides a useful chronological account of events.

Cooper, Michael. *The Japanese Mission to Europe, 1582-1590: The Journey of Four Samurai Boys through Portugal, Spain and Italy* (Folkestone: Global Oriental, 2005).

> Although the available sources are almost entirely limited to Catholic records, Cooper presents a lively and humanistic account of the Tenshō legation.

Hesselink, Reinier H. *The Dream of Christian Nagasaki: World Trade and the Clash of Cultures, 1560-1640* (Jefferson: McFarland, 2016).

> While the episodic structure makes it hard to grasp the overall narrative, the author has read deeply into original sources and the book contains a mine of information on the period.

Oka, Mihoko. *The Namban Trade: Merchants and Missionaries in 16th and 17th Century Japan* (Leiden: Brill, 2021).

A collection of essays on the organization of European trade in East Asia with a special focus on Macao. The author also provides background on trends in Japanese historiography.

Screech, Timon. *The Shogun's Silver Telescope: God, Art, and Money in the English Quest for Japan, 1600–1625* (Oxford: Oxford University Press, 2020).

A highly readable account of the English East India Company in Japan with an emphasis on trade, gift diplomacy, and the anti-Catholic machinations of the Company's merchants. The book is especially notable for its discussion of paintings, pottery, and other material culture.

## The Catholic Mission in Japan

Arimura, Rie. "The Catholic Architecture of Early Modern Japan: Between Adaptation and Christian Identity," *Japan Review* 27 (2014): 53–76.

Analysis of the evidence for Christian churches and other buildings.

Breen, John, and Mark Williams, eds. *Japan and Christianity: Impacts and Responses* (Basingstoke: Macmillan, 1996).

A wide-ranging collection of papers on the period.

Elison, George. *Deus Destroyed: The Image of Christianity in Early Modern Japan* (Cambridge, MA: Harvard University Press, 1973).

Influential study of the rejection of Christianity by the early modern Japanese state by Lithuanian-born scholar Jurgis Elisonas.

Ucerler, M. Antoni J. *The Samurai and the Cross: The Jesuit Enterprise in Early Modern Japan* (Oxford: Oxford University Press, 2022).

Comprehensive study of the period with extensive interpretation and analysis of original sources.

## Violence and Warfare

Chase, Kenneth. *Firearms: A Global History to 1700* (Cambridge: Cambridge University Press, 2003).

> Useful overview with a chapter on Japan and Korea.

Ogawa, Morihiro, ed. *Art of the Samurai: Japanese Arms and Armor, 1156–1868* (New York: Metropolitan Museum of Art, 2009).

> Lavishly illustrated catalogue which includes discussion of European influences on Japanese armour.

## Women in the Christian Century

Broomhall, Susan. *Evangelizing Korean Women and Gender in the Early Modern World: The Power of Body and Text* (Leeds: Arc Humanities Press, 2023).

> An important monograph on Christianity and Korean women, focusing especially on captives brought back to Japan after Hideyoshi's invasions.

Ward, Haruko. *Women Religious Leaders in Japan's Christian Century, 1549–1650* (Farnham: Ashgate, 2009).

> A path-breaking study of the role of women in the Christian Century.

## Japanese Colonialism between the Sixteenth and Seventeenth Centuries

Marino, Giuseppe, and Rebekah Clements. "Iberian sources on the Imjin war: the *Relação do fim e remate que teve a guerra da Corea* (1599)." *Sungkyun Journal of East Asian Studies* 23 (2023): 27–48.

> Analysis of a Jesuit source on Japan's invasion of Korea provides detailed background on the war and how it was perceived by Europeans.

Takakura, Shinichirō. "The Ainu of Northern Japan: A Study in Conquest and Acculturation," *Transactions of the American Philosophical Society* 50 (1960): 3–88.

> Annotated translation by John Harrison of a study by the most influential historian of Japan's colonial rule over Hokkaido. While Takakura's comparative approach to colonialism is focused (sometimes unconvincingly) on North America, his long article contains a great deal of useful information and analysis.

## Slavery

De Sousa, Lúcio. *The Portuguese Slave Trade in Early Modern Japan: Merchants, Jesuits and Japanese, Chinese and Korean Slaves* (Leiden: Brill, 2019).

> A wide-ranging work which includes much useful information on early European encounters with Japan. Short biographies of over four hundred slaves provide human details on the trade.

## Food and Foodways

Ishige, Naomichi. *The History and Culture of Japanese Food* (London: Kegan Paul, 2001).

> The most detailed overview in English on premodern Japanese foodways.

Laufer, Berthold. "The American Plant Migration. Part I: The Potato," *Anthropological Series, Field Museum of Natural History* 28 (1938).

> Remains the most comprehensive account in English of the spread of the potato to Japan.

Roullier, C., L. Benoit, D. B. McKey, and V. Lebot. "Historical Collections Reveal Patterns of Diffusion Sweet Potato in Oceania Obscured by Modern Plant Movements and recombination," *Proceedings of the National Academy of Sciences USA* 110 (2013): 2205–10.

> Combines botanical, archaeological and linguistic data to plot the early spread of sweet potato across the Pacific.

Schilling, Dorotheus. "Der erste Tabak in Japan," *Monumenta Nipponica* 5 (1942): 113–43.

> Study of documentary sources on the introduction of tobacco to Japan.

## Treponemal Disease

Salmon, Marylynn. *Medieval Syphilis and Treponemal Disease* (Leeds: Arc Humanities Press, 2022).

> An up-to-date overview of the history of treponemal disease based on skeletal, DNA, and documentary sources.

Suzuki, Takeo. *Palaeopathological and Palaeoepidemiological Study of Osseous Syphilis in Skulls of the Edo Period.* Tokyo: University Museum, University of Tokyo, Bulletin No. 23, 1984.

> Detailed bioarchaeological study of syphilis in early modern Japan.

## Crypto-Christians

Delakorda Kawashima, Tinka. "The Authenticity of the Hidden Christians' Villages in Nagasaki: Issues in the Evaluation of Cultural Landscapes." *Sustainability* 13 (2021): e4387.

> Analyses the crypto-Christian cultural landscape in terms of national and global policies in heritage protection.

Turnbull, Stephen. *The Kakure Kirishitan of Japan: A Study of their Development, Beliefs and Rituals to the Present Day* (Richmond: Curzon, 1998).

> Ethnohistoric study of the crypto-Christians emphasizing the role of syncretic popular religion.

## Japan and the Post-Reformation Church

Hsia, Adrian, and Ruprecht Wimmer, eds. *Mission und The-ater: Japan und China auf den Bühnen der Gessellschaft Jesu* (Regensburg: Schnell and Steiner, 2005).

> Collection of essays in German and English on representations of Japan and China in Jesuit plays, focusing on German-speaking Europe.

Joby, Christopher. *The Dutch Language in Japan (1600–1900): A Cultural and Sociolinguistic Study of Dutch as a Contact Language in Tokugawa and Meiji Japan* (Leiden: Brill, 2020).
    Exhaustive study of the impact of a European language in early modern Japan.

Oba, Haruka, Akihiko Watanabe, and Florian Schaffenrath, eds. *Japan on the Jesuit Stage: Transmissions, Receptions, and Regional Contexts* (Leiden: Brill, 2020).
    Extends and updates the coverage in *Mission und Theater*.

Printed in the United States
by Baker & Taylor Publisher Services